CHUCK JONES

PORTRAITS OF AMERICAN GENIUS

We are a people.
A people do not throw their geniuses away.
And if they are thrown away, it is our duty
as artists and as witnesses for the future
to collect them again for the sake of our children,
and, if necessary, bone by bone.

Alice Walker

Chuck Jones

A FLURRY OF DRAWINGS

Hugh Kenner

UNIVERSITY OF CALIFORNIA PRESS   BERKELEY   LOS ANGELES   LONDON

University of California Press
Berkeley and Los Angeles, California

University of California Press, Ltd.
London, England

© 1994 by
The Regents of the University of
California

Library of Congress
Cataloging-in-Publication Data
Kenner, Hugh.
  Chuck Jones : a flurry of drawings /
Hugh Kenner.
     p.   cm.—(Portraits of American
  genius ; 3)
  Includes bibliographical references
and index.
  ISBN 0-520-08797-6 (alk. paper)
  1. Jones, Chuck,
1912–   —Criticism and
interpretation.
  I. Jones, Chuck, 1912–
II. Title.   III. Series.
  NC1766.U52J6635 1994
  741.5'8'092—dc20   93-48418
                              CIP

Illustrations reprinted by permission
of the artist. © 1994 Chuck Jones
Enterprises.

Printed in the United States of
America
9 8 7 6 5 4 3 2 1

For Harry McCracken

CONTENTS

C huck Jones had a great-uncle Lynn who used to tell him that a pig could not be made into a racehorse. What might reasonably be hoped for, he said, was "a mighty fast pig."

So postulate a kid born, 1912, in Spokane. Endow him with a directionless passion for drawing. Enroll him in what was available, Chouinard Art Institute, in Los Angeles of all places, at a time when L.A. was a parvenu's paradise, a cultural desert. Next—1930—plunge the world into economic despair. Sit back, wait. No, do not expect a Malibu Leonardo. But, should genes and fortune and circumstance conspire just so, you may be rewarded with a surprising version of Uncle Lynn's "mighty fast pig."

Such is one approach to Charles Martin (Chuck) Jones, indisputably a master in an art—he'd have called it a trade— that only now is starting to be defined. That was motion picture Character Animation, and it flourished in one place in the world—Southern California—for perhaps thirty years (say 1933–63). Its several dozen practitioners (or several hundred; definitions are elastic) had the good fortune never to be aware that they were practicing anything resembling an art. (Otherwise put: neither did Animation Critics exist, nor were any Traditions easy to lay hold of.) It flourished thanks to economic givens that ought to have made anything of lasting interest impossible. Then it faded amid paeans to social progress. (And the brief flowering of Periclean Athens: was that perhaps equally chancy? We simply do not know how such things happen.)

Chuck Jones, 81 at this writing and going strong, now finds himself firmly installed in Animation History, a domain of learning that commenced to flourish less than two decades ago. One early instance is the January–February 1975 issue of *Film Comment.* Another is Jay Cocks's "The World that Jones Made," in the December 17, 1973, issue of *Time.* Though generous to Jones's way with studio properties—Bugs Bunny, Daffy Duck—Cocks drew special attention to the glorious one-shots: *One Froggy Evening,* notably; and *Duck Amuck,* which the priesthood is now about ready to call "self-reflexive." Should you ever face the solemn task of preserving just one six-minute instance from the unthinkable thousands of hours of animated footage that's accumulated since—oh, since 1914, you'd not go wrong in selecting "a Jones."

To savor such wonders you need to examine them repeatedly; and as long as they existed only on film, high cost kept access restricted to affluent fanatics. A like situation obtained in the long centuries when books were accessible solely via manuscript copies, too expensive for individuals to dream of. Today the video cassette recorder permits most of us to own the classics of animation, and certainly the finest work of Chuck Jones, at the total cost of a dinner or two or three on the town. For whatever purposes the VCR may have been marketed, friends of animation at least may perceive its worth. It's one more prizeworthy mighty fast pig.

The Jay Cocks article first alerted me to Chuck Jones. A letter to Cocks fetched a Jones address; then a letter to Jones brought Jones to Baltimore, where, one memorable afternoon and evening, he discoursed, drew pictures for children, and showed a Johns Hopkins audience a film anthology. The texture of the discourse was memorable; I wish I could recall who it was he characterized as "a trellis of varicose veins." And the films—I'll not forget Arnold Stein the Milton scholar, inclining his head after *One Froggy Evening* to confide, "That was simple . . . and AB-so-lute."

As it was.

At Corona del Mar, California, in July 1990, I saw Chuck and Marian Jones daily for a week. What got taped on those visits is a primary source for this book. Though I've since tried to cross-check facts, I can't guarantee them. Animation history remains rife with vagaries of human memory. Meanwhile it seems worth setting down what I can offer.

A word about printed sources. In addition to the January–February 1975 *Film Comment,* and one article in a later issue (May–June 1976), I've drawn on Jones's own 1989 memoir *Chuck Amuck,* on Steve Schneider's 1988 *That's All Folks!: The Art of Warner Bros. Animation,* on Joe Adamson's 1990 *Bugs Bunny: Fifty Years and Only One Grey Hare,* and on John Grant's *Encyclopedia of Walt Disney's Animated Characters* (second edition, 1992). I've not meticulously acknowledged every use, partly to keep footnote clutter thinned out, partly because my most frequent recourse to a book or an article was for cross-checking something I'd heard from Chuck Jones. Like all great raconteurs he tends to have formulaic versions of key stories, and when what I heard was almost word for word what another interviewer had heard I felt under no obligation to dwell on the fact.

Four people I've never met helped make this book possible. Jennifer Jumper in Seattle was heroic in transcribing tapes riddled with nonsense such as airplane noises. Dave Mackey in Oakhurst, New Jersey, made a key video available and has since answered flurries of queries. Paul Raulerson in Eagan, Minnesota, explicated the computer's way of handling a comma. And Harry McCracken in Arlington, Massachusetts, put at my disposal his tape library and his vast knowledge of Animation History. I'm in touch with the four of them thanks to a computer network: the Byte Information Exchange (BIX). We enjoy a high-tech age and ought to acknowledge it.

—H.K.
August 1993

All the illustrations in this book were drawn by Chuck Jones. They are reproduced, with his permission, from his informal autobiography, *Chuck Amuck,* and from a model sheet he designed to guide the animators of *Rikki-Tikki-Tavi.*

More important are the key Jones films on VCR tapes. If you've trouble finding them locally, a phone call (Monday–Saturday, 9 A.M.–6 P.M. Pacific time) to (206) 441-4130 will fetch you the *Whole Toon Catalog,* and what Whole Toon can't find it's a good bet nobody can.

A nimation, like life itself, relies on natural principles. Life requires simply (simply!) DNA. Animation requires Persistence of Vision. That means: anything you've glimpsed you'll go on seeing for maybe a tenth of a second after it's gone. If meanwhile a different glimpse gets substituted, the two will blend smoothly. And if they depict successive stages of movement, you'll swear you saw something move.

Ways to substitute the next image derive from flip-books, which have been around since at least the nineteenth century. On the bottom margin of a school scribbler, a sketch of a car. On successive pages, the same car, shifted incrementally rightward. Now. Riffle the pages! Watch that auto move!

To check what they've done, animators riffle stacks of pages. No single drawing stands out. Single drawings, however highly finished, may at best—Chuck Jones says—serve to help us remember some animated sequence we recall enjoying. But Animation itself: Jones calls that "a flurry of drawings." How they're shown is less important than their flurry. A flip-book can display a couple of seconds' worth. For something longer, best photograph each frame; then let a projector sequence them on a screen, fast enough for Persistence of Vision to blend them. Sixteen frames per second was fast enough in silent-film days. Sound, when it came about 1928, required twenty-four because film that carried sound had to move faster. But the eye doesn't need that many; twelve per second will do for the eye. So sound helped ease the animator's lot. Instead of sixteen drawings per second, twelve will suffice, each photographed twice. The eye will detect no jerkiness.

A flurry of drawings: one by one by one. Draw the starting pose; then draw the next instant, then the next, clear to the end of this flurry, each image a modified tracing of the one before it: that's called "animating straight-ahead," and it's how all animation was done for a couple of decades, right into the age of sound, sixteen for each second. In 1914, Winsor McCay's many thousand straight-ahead drawings made Gertie the Dinosaur huff, stomp, lower her neck. Chuck Jones, as he likes to remark, was then two years old. "It all happened within my lifetime." (And McCay, born 1871, lived till 1934; by then Jones, 22, had enjoyed three years of breathing animation's ozone.)

McCay redrew every detail of every frame: not only Gertie, who'd shift from glimpse to glimpse, but also all those things that shouldn't shift: rocks, mountains, trees, horizon. Retracing those with machine-like accuracy being simply impossible even for his (or his assistant's) steady hand, they flickered and shimmered around Gertie. In its time, the effect did seem rather charming. But what a redundancy of effort! A way to draw a background once, for reuse many dozen times, was one thing that would raise animation above slave labor. It would also permit something later to prove indispensable in establishing a world (stable) that contained characters (a-move). That was a perfectly unambiguous distinction between what was meant to stay rock-steady and what wasn't.

Not that McCay's audiences needed that distinction. When he took his film on tour, and stood beside the screen with a pointer to conduct dialogues with Gertie, many were unclear that they were looking at drawings. Some kind of real animal, surely, though oddly drained of color? Or maybe some kind of model? It's hard to realize how long we can take simply learning to perceive a novel medium. (How about a voice in your head, with no one else in the room? When a prominent Boston lawyer heard the "telephone" demonstrated about 1876, well, after pausing long in embarrassment he came up with nothing better than "Rig a jig, and away we go!")[1]

Nor would slave labor have entered McCay's thoughts. Like many pioneer animators, he was driven by a passion for drawing. To make a hundred pictures in a morning, that was sheer heaven!

We're talking of a gone time of linked passions. Moviegoers had a passion too, for nothing more subtle than the sheer illusion of motion. It sufficed that on a wavery screen they saw—galloping horses! (And therein lay the germ of the Western.) Chuck Jones remembers when it was hilarious

---

1. It was Bell's assistant, the famed Mr. Watson, who recorded this. See Avital Ronell, *The Telephone Book* (1991), pp. 227 ff.

if an animated walker just hopped once in a while, an effect he's used himself in several films. A story? That could emerge from whatever some animator happened to think of next.

(And to keep things steadily lined up, put a row of pegs on the table, to fit holes along an edge of what's being photographed. Raoul Barre thought of that in 1914. Every cel, every sheet of animators' paper, has worn those holes ever since.)

The reusable-background problem was solved, after several fumbles, in 1914: U.S. Patent #1,143,542, issued to Earl Hurd. His solution wasn't obvious, discarding as it did the natural supposition that the drawings the camera would see would be the ones drawn on paper. No. Draw the background—once—on paper. Then trace each of your "moving" drawings onto celluloid. Under the camera, lay each "cel" in sequence over the background; click the button for each. Voilà!

That process created two new occupations: cel-tracer, cel-washer. The tracers have now mostly been automated out, and a good thing too, since, careful though they might be, they lost subtleties. Run Jones's *How the Grinch Stole Christmas* on your VCR; examine the wiggly lines that delineate the Grinch's haggard face in closeup; no way those wiggles could have been reliably traced. By Grinch-time (1966) an unwavering Xerox eye was transferring the animator's every nuanced line to the cel. (Opaque areas—after color came in, colored ones—got painted inside the outlines by hand, and still are.) And the washers? Their job was to permit reuse of precious celluloid, by cleaning the paint off cels that had been photographed. Chuck Jones, at 19, commenced his long life in animation as a cel-washer.

He'd been hired by Ub Iwerks of the (yes) Dutch name, and who was Ub? Ubbe Ert Iwerks, who'd come west in 1924 to rejoin his Kansas City partner Walt Disney. They were both 23. It's no secret that Ub's drawing was more resourceful than Walt's; that he co-created Mickey Mouse; that he, single-handed, animated the pioneer Mickey cartoons, notably the 1928 *Steamboat Willie*. That was the cartoon that made history with fully synchronized sound, thanks to Walt's nigh-infallible nose for trends. By 1930 an entrepreneur named Patrick Powers had persuaded Ub (wrongly) that he was more important than Walt, and set him up in a studio of his own. Ub proceeded to produce films starring Flip the Frog, who flopped. He had, alas, Chuck Jones recalls, "no sense of humor." That was a considerable drawback.

Ub Iwerks did excel at technical challenges. When Flip climbed a stair the viewer's eye climbed with him, so the stair's perspective shifted with every frame. That called for ultra-resourceful animating.

Later, back with Disney, Ub would tinker with such things as Xeroxing cels instead of hand-tracing them, and with processes for achieving a seamless blend of live action and animation. (There seems to be no substance to printed reports that he fathered Disney's Multiplane project, the camera looking down through widely-spaced cels to automate shifts of perspective as viewpoints shifted. True, he worked on such an apparatus. But the long opening shot of *Pinocchio*, a Multiplane tour de force of 1940, preceded Ub's return to Disney.)

Anyhow, in 1931, with an infusion of cash, Tycoon Iwerks had been on his own; hiring the likes of cel-washers; also importing from the east animators of the quality of Grim Natwick.

"Grim" is said to be what he'd uttered as a toddler, trying to pronounce his real name, which was Myron. Born 1890, and not gone till after he'd passed his hundredth birthday—Lord, like symphony conductors, animators are long-lived!—Grim Natwick had commenced animating as far back as 1916, for the Pathé Studio in New York, where he'd finish eight dozen straight-ahead drawings before his lunch break. Later, with the Max Fleischer people, he laid claim to what then didn't look like immortality by creating Betty Boop, at first a little dog with spit curls that walked on its hind legs to perform a Boop-boop-a-doop vocal identified with a singer named Helen Kane. (In those early days of sound, animating pop hits was one sure cartoon formula.) By three more films the dog's droopy ears had become earrings, and Betty was, well, Betty. Grim Natwick was the envy of other Fleischer animators because he could join Betty's hand to her arm with a wrist; could even manage knees. That was because he'd had formal art-school training. Most animators, then and for decades to come, learned their craft by merely tracing photographs. When photos weren't available, the arms and legs they drew evaded knees and elbows by bending like rubber hoses.

(Tracing photos, a technique much exploited by the Fleischers, is still known as "rotoscoping." It's a way to get a quick fix on humans, who can be filmed in action as no Bugs Bunny can be. It is widely regarded as cheating. It was also a way to manage *Snow White*'s wooden prince, rightly noted as that landmark film's principal lapse. Yes, action footage of a girl walking and dancing—the model would become better known as Marge Champion—was studied by the animators of the princess, but those frames weren't for tracing. In changing her overall height from eight heads to five, Hamil-

ton Luske, the man in charge, detached her from human pro- 7
portions and her artisans from tracery.)

And, long before Snow White was thought of, here's Grim Natwick, 41, at the Ub Iwerks studio. And here's a 19-year-old cel-washer, Charles M. Jones, equipped, like Grim, with a species of formal art-school training. And (Grim would recall) "I took him out, bought him an ice cream soda, and taught him all about crooked lines." Ah, esoterica!

Eventually—the details are elusive—Chuck Jones became Grim's Assistant Animator.

That sounds more grandiose than it was. Assistant Animators were earlier dubbed "In-betweeners," and their craft, like cel-washing, depended on a technical advance. That was the observation that if animators drew key poses—a left foot hitting the ground, a right foot ditto—then the frames in between, the ones that shifted the walker from left foot to right foot, could be as routine to draw as they were to walk, and might as well be assigned to anyone with the skill just to draw at all. (Standards would rise, but that was the way it looked then.) "How fast is the walk?" would translate into "How many in-between frames?"—an instruction the animator could relay. That was the end of straight-ahead animation. Thenceforward, Key Poses and In-betweening By the Numbers. As a dividend, a bright In-betweener might be learning to animate. Most animators of the Jones generation and since have learned their craft In-betweening. (Also, a few In-betweeners have been discerned who seem happy to use up their lives just In-betweening. Chuck Jones doesn't pretend to understand them.)

It all made economic sense too. Animators were freed for uniquely productive work, while In-betweening could be left to the peons. For a labor-intensive industry had long been

A Flurry of Drawings

sorting out its skills. Someone (Disney, Fleischer, Iwerks) in charge at the top. A few key creative people—Animators. Eager In-betweeners, making maybe nine-tenths of the drawings. A background artist or two. And a phalanx of anonymous inkers and painters, to fuss with the cels the camera would actually see. And, no, don't forget the cameraman; we need him. And some folk to whomp up the sound. Oh—don't forget the story either. We'll return to that.

And what, really, was it all about? That depends on the angle from which we calibrate "really." What the moguls saw—we'll start with them—was money (not much) dribbled out to gaggles of odd people, in return for some hand-drawn footage every week or two. Back when just seeing something move was a delight, audiences had formed the habit of expecting such footage; thus a novelty had become a program fixture. By the 1920s the Pat Sullivan studio, which was mostly Otto Messmer,[2] was affording audiences a routine fix with Felix the Cat, the first clear-cut instance of Character Animation. (Gertie? She'd been a prop for the real character, her creator.)

Felix, whom Messmer cannily reduced to some brushable blobs, routinely stalked, pondered, triumphed. "I put emphasis on personality in Felix," Messmer would recall: "eye motion and facial expressions." He'd long since discovered he could "get as big a laugh with a little gesture—a wink or a twist of the tail"—as he could with gags. That meant, he'd created a Character: an emblem audiences could invest with expectations, disappointments, triumphs. It's unknown how

2. Died 1982, aged 91. Note the pattern of longevity.

many Felix films got made, several hundred anyhow, and an effort to remember that they all preceded sound. It was also a symptom of emergent custom that O. Messmer's name wasn't credited, just Pat Sullivan's. Pat Sullivan was the Producer, i.e., the financial liaison. But he even got himself photographed as if his days were spent animating.

Sound brought in a new stimulus: music. Audiences could now stomp their feet. And studios tended to own music companies. Warner Bros. owned perhaps six. Aha! Such eyes as Jack Warner's lit up with dollar-signs! Music could bring continuity to Looney Tunes, and the cartoons could help sell the music. For several years that seemed a primary reason to make cartoons. "When I was young," Chuck Jones remembers, "music publishing was a big business because . . . oh, people played the ukulele." (Nowadays, adept with chords on the guitar, many strummers feel no need for sheet music.)

Sound was in some ways a regression: would a hallful of foot-stompers ever miss Character? But yes, a demand persisted for Mickey Mouse, whom Disney and Iwerks had created just when sound was dawning. So for years the Disney output was bifurcated—in alternate fortnights, a Mickey Mouse (character), a Silly Symphony (foot-stomp). Luckily, Walt Disney came to see the Silly Symphonys as carte blanche to just play around. Playing around can pay off. May 1933 saw a turning point in animation history. That was a Silly Symphony called *The Three Little Pigs*.

In the mid-thirties it was a sensation, a cartoon that went on playing week after week while features came and went behind it. After fifty years it remains amazing. A governing tune—

A Flurry of Drawings

Who's afraid of the Big Bad Wolf
Big Bad Wolf
Big Bad Wolf

keeps two pigs a-hopping and a-fluting and a-fiddling while a Practical Pig lays bricks.

And they Hop and they Flute and they Fiddle *tweedle dee* and Again and Again *fiddle fie fee fee* and the Wolf jumps **WHOMP** and they Gallop and they Stomp as their Practical friend can see.

The third pig's rhythms are prosaic compared to theirs; diddle diddle diddle diddle isn't his life style. At bottom it's the old theme of the Ant and the Grasshopper, the Ant thoughtful for tomorrow (a wolf may arrive at the door), the Grasshopper incorrigibly *toujours gai.*

Chuck Jones compares Walt's founding of the Disney Studios with the founding of the *New Yorker* by Harold Ross at about the same period. If Ross was no great writer, neither was Walt a great animator. But each created a milieu in which greatness could flourish. And greatness, insofar as it's attachable to animation, undoubtably attaches to *The Three Little Pigs,* three characters (says Jones) who are characterized solely by the way they move, since they *look* exactly alike. (Before that, he adds, villains were heavy, victims not. That simple distinction continued into the days of Bluto and Popeye.) Unique selfness, inherent in a way of moving: that is the essence of the Character Animation we're keeping track of. Reality inheres in rhythm.

So yes, yes, things were happening backstage, not always beknownst to studios like MGM and Warners which owned chains of theaters, by the early 1930s all "wired for sound."

A Flurry of Drawings

Into their theaters they dumped their two-hour "product." That meant, more or less, a ninety-minute feature every week, plus a newsreel, plus a two-reeler, plus a cartoon. A reel is about nine minutes. Cartoons got shaved to seven minutes, then to six. But, however brief, a cartoon there had to be. Lacking it, the package would have seemed short-weighted.

In a way, it's as simple as that. Hence all those flurries of drawings.

n 1912 the *Titanic* sank, a man named Funk coined the word "vitamin," Robert Scott reached the South Pole, "Piltdown Man" was exhumed, Jim Joyce turned thirty, and Sam Beckett six. Also New Mexico was admitted to the Union (hence Bugs Bunny's formulaic "Left turn at Albuquerque"; and later the roadrunner, *Geococcyx californianus,* would become New Mexico's state bird). Moreover, the 1912 autumnal equinox—21 September, a Saturday—saw Charles Martin (Chuck) Jones born in Spokane.

That year was pre-TV, pre-cinema, even pre-radio. (Yes, wireless and movies existed, but no, they didn't dominate the time of any folk save tech fanatics.) That left, well, *books,* so if you felt unsleepy your recourse was reading. It was also your rainy-day recourse, and, when necessary, your way of cocooning yourself when you were the third of four and your siblings were, all three, assertive. ("Margaret Barbara Jones, master weaver and designer, teacher and fabric designer;

Dorothy Jane Jones, sculptor, writer, and illustrator; Richard Kent Jones, painter, photographer, teacher, and printmaker": that's the roll-call that also includes "Charles Martin Jones, animator and animated-cartoon director.")[1]

He was formed by literacy and is still focused on it. In the heat of discourse he'll drop a phrase from a book every few sentences, and frequently pause to credit it. In his wonderful memoir, *Chuck Amuck,* he recalls a long-ago cat named Johnson uttering "a single laconic 'Mckgnaow.'" A footnote credits James Joyce's *Ulysses,* "but Johnson said it first." Now what Leopold Bloom's hungry cat said that Dublin June morning was something slightly different: "Mkgnao."[2] The point is, Jones is quoting from memory, something the truly literate have the confidence to do. He was writing a book that doesn't pretend to scholarship, and felt no special impulse to reach for the shelf, flip pages, verify. His points get made: Johnson, an authentic cat, spoke authentic cat-speech, and Joyce, an authentic writer, got cat-speech right. As does Jones, thanks to the real Johnson reinforcing Joycean fiction the way (as Joyce fans will verify) reality normally does.

Chuck Jones insists on the reliability of authentic writers. Here's Mark Twain on the coyote: "The coyote is a long, slim, sick and sorry-looking skeleton, with a gray wolf-skin stretched over it, a tolerably bushy tail that forever sags down with a despairing expression of forsakenness and misery, a furtive and evil eye, and a long sharp face with a

1. *Chuck Amuck,* p. 45.
2. And with further urgency, "Mrkgnao!" and "Mrkrgnao!" Readers in need of rigorous detail about feline vocal resources should consult Muriel Beadle, *The Cat* (1977), pp. 186–8.

CAT AND SYLVESTER

THE EARS DO LOOK SOMETHING ALIKE
EVEN THOUGH THERE IS A PAINFUL
DISCREPANCY IN THE NOSES.

RABBIT —

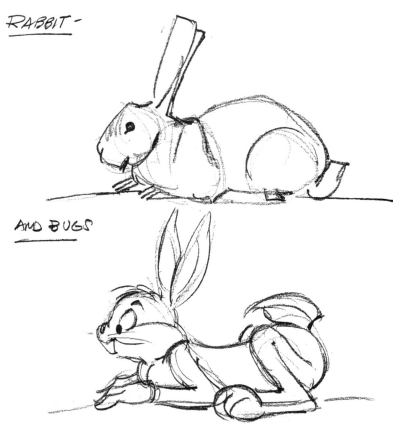

AND BUGS

THIS IS NO MORE A NATURAL
POSITION FOR BUGS THAN IT
WOULD BE FOR A HUMAN BEING
— BUT, I'M TRYING TO BE FAIR.

COYOTE

WILE E. COYOTE

VITAL DIFFERENCE: WILE E.'S EYES ARE BLOOD SHOT.

it because he had to help support his family. So by 25 he'd become railroad yardmaster in San Francisco, from which his next move was to Panama, where they had their minds on a Canal. "Both my sisters were born in the Panama Canal Zone. And I was conceived there, but born in Spokane, Washington. I never forgave him for that. It's much more elegant to say you were born in Panama, at least I thought so—in the tropics." Father, "a sort of Richard Harding Davis," loved the idea of living in the tropics. So he always dressed in white and wore boots. "God, he was a good-looking, beautiful, handsome man."

Mother? Mabel McQuiddy Martin, "born in a place called Nevada, Missouri." Pronounce that Ne-*vay*-da. And raised in Schnute, Kansas, where she was "belle of the town." Charles Adams Jones came there to visit a friend, spotted the belle, "hired a pair of spanking bays and a carriage with the fringe on top, swept her off her feet, took her away for a honeymoon in New York and then down to Panama." Next, Metropolitan Life hired C.A.J. to manage its northwest territory; hence the move to Spokane just before the birth of our Charles Martin, who bears his father's first name and his mother's maiden name and goes by "Chuck." C.A.J. didn't like living in Spokane, any more than his son was to relish having been born there instead of in Panama, "so much more elegant to say." So Jones Sr. "headed for Southern California, and that was the last of being wealthy. He kept starting new businesses and failing." And the kids had all that Hammermill Bond to use for drawing-paper, and all those pencils. "I think all kids will draw if they're encouraged to do so" is Chuck's answer to a question about where the talent may have come from. Encouragement, doubtless, is part of the story. But also there was their mother's attitude:

Termite Terrace

"She was willing to make the sacrifice most parents will not make: she would not criticize, and she would not over-praise. Years later she told me that if we brought a drawing to her, she didn't look at the drawing, she looked at us. And if we seemed to be excited, then she would be excited. But if I just brought a drawing for, you know, just because, then she would look at it . . . and she would never say 'What's that?' or 'Is that Daddy?' or anything like that. She would look at it and say, 'My, you used a lot of blue, didn't you?'

"No criticism. Also no over-praise. Praise probably hurts more than anything else. You come running over with a drawing, and they say, 'Oh, that's wonderful,' and stick it up on the refrigerator. After a while the child says, 'Look, I know all my drawings aren't good.' And loses interest because, obviously, the parent had lost interest."

Chuck Jones was 15 when he entered Chouinard after not graduating from high school, and in the time he spent there he had no glimmer of the use to which he'd one day be putting the anatomy they were teaching him. His stint of cel-washing at the Ub Iwerks establishment (1931) came after some futile months at a commercial art studio, where he was dogged (he says) by a post-Chouinard inability to draw. (Subsequently, he hastens to add, ten years of night school and "the great teacher Donald Graham" would enable him to claim that if he still can't draw he can fake it pretty well. As he assuredly can.)

In 1933, following a distinct lack of success as a freelance portrait sketcher at $1 per, Chuck Jones made the move of his life, to Leon Schlesinger Productions. Schlesinger had previously headed something called Pacific Art and Title, the principal product of which was the dialogue cards on which silent films depended. (The heroine's lips move; then a card: "Oh, Henry . . . I hear . . . *horses!*") A feature might use several dozen of those, or up to several hundred. But now that there were soundtracks, audiences could *hear* the heroine's voice, and the future for dialogue cards seemed bleak. Schlesinger, ever canny, saw how to cut his dependence on cards. He cooked up a three-way deal. He would back a couple of artists named Hugh Harman and Rudolph Ising, sometime Disney associates, to crank out a cartoon a month; the cartoons in turn he would market to Warner Bros., who would use them to promote songs from their feature films and their sheet-music companies. Thus cash would flow from the Warners to Schlesinger, who would pass no more than he had to back to Harman-Ising[4] while reserving the rest for necessities such as his yacht. Thus the Looney Tunes were born, and if you think that name carries an echo of Silly Symphonys you are right. The first Looney Tune, *Sinkin' in the Bathtub,* opened in a Warner-owned theater on Broadway, May 6, 1930. Its star was a li'l ol' black boy named Bosko, and finger-pointers should pause to recall the technical constraints of an era when *all* cartoon stars were apt to be black: Felix the Cat, Flip the Frog, yes, Mickey Mouse himself. A body you could fill in fast with a brush: that was a great help when you had to turn out hundreds upon hundreds of nigh-identical drawings. (Also, Bosko exploited the tradition of Al Jolson's blackface *Jazz Singer,* the pioneer talkie and a Warner Bros. production.) A year and a half later, Warners commissioned a second series, called Merrie Melodies. Those were conceived as one-shots, meant to market Warner songs, and

4. And here it's routine to remark a lovely pairing of names.

for several years every Merrie Melodie was required to contain "at least one complete chorus of a Warner-owned tune."

Harman and Ising had ideas of quality that Leon Schlesinger didn't want to finance, and eventually they terminated the deal and took Bosko with them to MGM. That left Schlesinger owning, as Steve Schneider puts it, "the rights to the phrases 'Looney Tunes,' 'Merrie Melodies,' and 'That's all, folks!' but with no staff and no known characters."[5] To maintain the cash flow from Warners he hadn't a recourse save to get a staff together. He took over a building on the old Warner lot, lured Friz Freleng and Bob Clampett back from Harman-Ising, and picked up from Disney a few men experienced enough to start in as Production Supervisors, later called Directors. It was in the midst of that turmoil that Charles M. Jones joined the staff: a sometime cel-washer whose in-betweening hadn't made Ub Iwerks think he was worth keeping around. If on some pages of *Chuck Amuck* the self-deprecation sounds a trifle formulaic, still it's easy to imagine how Jones could have felt that the Warner cartoon operation acquired him, somehow, by mistake. He would stay with it for three productive decades.

Meanwhile, a wonderful plot twist. The second time Chuck Jones was terminated by the Iwerks enterprise (no, you don't need the details; Ub let him go, he sneaked back in, was fired again; it all happened in a few weeks of 1931)— well, the second firing was performed by Ub's secretary, Dorothy Webster, a sociology graduate (U. of Oregon). The ways of courtship being extraterrestial, in 1935 that same Dorothy Webster became Mrs. Charles M. Jones, and in 1937

---

5. Steve Schneider, *That's All Folks!* (1988), p. 40.

mother to Linda Jones, who today, as Linda Jones Clough, runs two companies called Linda Jones Enterprises and Chuck Jones Enterprises, of which a principal activity is "producing, preserving and authenticating drawings and cels from my past, present and future, selling them through major art galleries in the United States." Dorothy Webster Jones, "friend, critic, writer, dance partner,[6] wonderful mother and grandmother," died in 1978. Five years later Chuck married Marian J. Dern, by profession a writer-photographer. He's been blissfully fortunate, twice.

It was Dorothy, he says, who somehow got him the job at Schlesinger's, back in the time of the breakaway from Harman-Ising. That put Chuck Jones in position to benefit by a major episode in animation history.

For in 1935, twenty-seven-year-old Fred ("Tex") Avery from Taylor, Texas, claiming to be a descendant of Judge Roy Bean, showed up at Schlesinger Productions. He said he'd directed two cartoons for Walter Lantz, though, Steve Schneider says, "no screen credits exist to that effect," and he somehow got put in charge of a new unit, staffed by men who weren't happy where they'd been. They included Chuck Jones, Bob Clampett, and "a terrific draftsman" named Bob ("Bobe") Cannon. About 1970 Avery was recalling them all as "tickled to death": "They wanted to get a 'new group' going, and 'we could do it' and 'let's make pictures.' It was very encouraging. . . . We worked every night. My gosh, nothing stopped us!" They were installed in a building of their own on the Warner lot—a white one-story bungalow,

6. A 1954 square-dance book, *Five Years of Sets in Order,* is introduced by Chuck Jones.

quickly dubbed Termite Terrace once the new crew became aware of other live beings around. Shamus Culhane would remember from his stint there in '43 a place that "looked and stank like the hold of a slave ship," and Michael Maltese, long-time storyman, remembered a colleague who "tried to set fire to it once, just for the hell of it, just to see if it burned. And it wouldn't burn." And before long, in that unlikely place, Chuck Jones, sometime cel-washer and in-betweener and quondam apprentice to Grim Natwick, was animating for Tex Avery.

For reasons that will appear, he couldn't have had a better mentor at just that point in his career. Avery's sense of the animatable universe was formed in the decade when a dotted line from the eye of Felix the Cat could knock over a chipmunk, and he remained impervious to any claim that animation should strive for the Illusion of Life. So an Avery squirrel shakes a boxing glove lest it contain a (shudder!) horseshoe, whereupon a full-sized horse tumbles out head-first, its expression blissfully bland. Or an Avery bit-player with "one foot in the grave" hobbles up to the bar with (in Joe Adamson's words) "an entire plot of ground, an erected tombstone and a decorative tulip all cumbersomely attached to the end of his right leg."[7] That kind of gag takes a couple of seconds; Adamson is right to emphasize that what's funny isn't really the gag, after all rather simple-minded if you think about it, but "the brazen vividness of the presentation." The days of Felix were gone; animation's universe had since been enriched with color, sound, copious detail; its inhabitants were no longer inky blobs. Even Mickey Mouse, at one time a

---

7. See Joe Adamson, *Tex Avery: King of Cartoons* (1975).

blackness with big white eyeballs and a pair of red shorts, had acquired, by the time of 1937's *Brave Little Tailor,* a jacket, a belt with a wallet, moreover a loop to carry scissors, all topped by a jaunty feathered hat with a turned-up brim. In so lavishly detailed a universe the mere dotted-line stare would need enhancing, perhaps with trumpets, raised curtains, centered spotlights.

All this craziness, Jones thought it worth emphasizing one morning, was dreamed up and executed by men in hats and ties and vests. "In those days, when you went to work you took off your coat, maybe, but very often you left your vest on. And if you loosened your tie, still you did not take it off." That describes men in uniform, so to speak.

Tex Avery stayed at Warners till Leon Schlesinger fired him in mid-1941 (their dispute was over the final forty feet of a film called *The Heckling Hare*), and Chuck Jones animated or helped animate seven Avery pictures, 1936–37. It's arguable that the truly mad and memorable Avery emerged at MGM, 1942–55. To that period belong, for example, the films, notably *Little Rural Riding Hood,* that feature a lecherous wolf (essentially, the Disney wolf of 1933, but no longer obsessed with just food) and a disarmingly human redheaded nightclub singer. She is animated with the chastest imaginable sexiness,[8] and he, on first sighting her from his table, invariably finds some eleven different ways to fly madly apart. Sheer libido, you understand, nothing to remark on, the world needs to be kept populated; still, it's hard to forget his eyes popping out two yards on taut strings, or his feet astomp on his head, or his body breaking up into five pieces which by some miraculous law snap back together.

---

8. And no rotoscopes were used, Joe Adamson assures us; nor was anyone so much as peeking at live-action footage.

As to what all this has to do with Chuck Jones, who as we've said animated for Avery during just two years, after which he was promoted to Supervisor (i.e., Director) on his own; well, it's perfectly true that Avery's style of boundless exaggeration was never Jones's. What Tex Avery did establish—though for Chuck Jones the lesson took time to stick—was simply the autonomy of the Director's created world. The world of the transcendent Jones cartoons—think of *One Froggy Evening* or *What's Opera, Doc?*—has no firm connections with any world outside itself. Humans, such as dicker with talent agents or use their life savings to hire theaters, coexist with a green frog who wears a top hat and sings "Hello, My Baby" and can also walk a tightrope. A pig who sings Wagner soon joins a rabbit who can play a ballerina in drag and can also slide down a white horse with the best of circus stars, in what the rabbit announces has been not opera but send-up ("What did you expect—a *happy* ending?"). It doesn't seem too much to say that Tex Avery's presence—though none of his major films got made at Warners—underlaid the great period when Warner cartoons, to the general bemusement of Warner brass, paced the cartoon industry, and also fostered Chuck Jones. Jones needed Avery's example. But Tex Avery had to get clear of Warners to flourish, and Jones could not have flourished anywhere else.

For a fix on this complicated theme, consider the role of Walt Disney Enterprises in a world where rival studios, and notably Warners, seemed to have no firm objective save not to be lavish with money. At WDE they came to know what they were after, and it wasn't what Avery was after, nor for that matter what the post-Avery Warners valued. What they were after *chez* Disney was the look of expensive perfection. Now define Perfection. (Clearing of executives' throats . . .)

Cartoons were for kids—right? Or so Walt Disney was thinking by about 1935. Thus at Burbank they made Silly Symphonys that would have been far better had they been sillier—a langorous Wynken, Blynken and Nod, for example, as cutey-cute cute as the wooden shoe of a starship they rode through the sky, dangling candy-cane hooks to catch stars. Mothers were meant to recall how *their* mothers had read Eugene Field's verses to them; were meant also to conclude that their own children would of course love what they themselves seemed to remember loving. Meanwhile the animators gave more and more attention to getting details like the swirl of waves Exactly Right. They'd even check their drawn efforts against live-action footage. When Frank Thomas and Ollie Johnston, two of Disney's "Nine Old Men," subtitled their big 1981 *Disney Animation* book "The Illusion of Life," they disclosed more than they perhaps meant to. Somehow, some time a little after the transcendent *Three Little Pigs,* the perfection Art seeks had been redefined at Disney. Artists were to try for something miscalled Realism, described at one point in the Thomas-Johnston book as "that rich look of a first-class illustration," which hints at, oh, gallery-quality Norman Rockwell.

Warner Bros. animation at its finest had no truck with any such Illusion of Life. But that would be later. At Warner Bros. in the 1930s, Chuck Jones says, Disney's doings were regarded with absolute awe, and by no one more than by Jones himself, who, once he became a director, worked through a long sticky period of Disney-worship. (Obvious how Chouinard training might encourage that. Attach a hand to an arm?

Ah, one more thing I know exactly how to do.) Early in the second half-century since *Tom Thumb in Trouble* (1940) was, as they say, "released," a viewer of that landmark film is hard put to distinguish admiration from embarrassment. "Supervision" is "by Charles M. Jones"; also credited is one animator, Robert Cannon, the "terrific draftsman" who'd been part of Avery's inheritance at Warners and who clearly had a fine grasp of how to portray the undistorted human form. It's, yes, beautifully drawn; and if you like a nice sentimental story, that's present too, thanks to storyman Rich Hogan (who would soon move to MGM and for years provide Tex Avery with his most Averyesque ideas, dancing redheads, exploding wolves.) But this story? To quote Jerry Beck and Will Friedwald's indispensable *Looney Tunes and Merrie Melodies,* "Once upon a time in the dark forest lived a woodchopper and his tiny son, Tom Thumb. Tom is so small that he can take a bath in his dad's cupped hands." A bird (we'll skip some details) saves Tom's life but Dad drives it away. Tom sets forth in a snowstorm to find it. And (quoting again), "Dad awakens and calls for his son. The little bird hears Dad's calls and flies to Tom, bringing him home. Dad, crying over the loss of his son, looks up to see Tom and the bird. That night, Tom is safely asleep in the pillow, the little bird nestled in Dad's beard." Treacle; *lachrymose* treacle, moreover. But it's all done with exemplary expertise. Astonishing, how the Warner folk could animate a big bearded human with slow but admirable realism, back when other studios (Disney, Fleischer) would prepare to do just that kind of thing by studying live-action footage such as Leon Schlesinger said he lacked the budget for.

Beck and Friedwald provide an interesting coda to their entry on *Tom Thumb in Trouble.* "Although the Warner cartoon staff had tried to mimic Disney in the past, by 1940 they had pretty much given up that ambition in favor of the gag approach with which they would soon achieve popular success. This film is a deliberate, last-time effort to figure out the Disney formula. Disney would be used only as a source of satire in the future."

"The gag approach" . . .: That phrase is unnecessarily blank, implying as it does adolescent disrespect for something we haven't the skills or the budget to emulate. And "the Disney formula": that depended, surely, less on Disney animation than on Disney marketing. Walt's narcotics were *safe* for the kiddies; whereas it's been routinely objected from that day to this that the Warner formula is *bad* for them, incorporating as it does so much **violence.** My first afternoon with Chuck Jones, in Baltimore, back in 1974, was punctuated by a woman with a Social Conscience who charged him with promulgating violence, *vide* those awful "Road Runners." Having heard that, oh, say, 8,053 times, Chuck wasn't deterred. The Coyote, he pointed out, is the only one who gets battered; but never, ever, does the Coyote find himself in a situation he didn't set up, personally and in detail. (Unmollified, Ms. Conscience, a lighter-into, next lit into the hors d'oeuvres.)

We're walking a delicate line. On the one hand, Jones is allegedly the maestro of mindless violence. (Wrong.) On the other hand, he's animation's stickiest sentimentalist. (Also Not Right, though Tex Avery is quoted as saying "That was almost a Jones" about a cartoon of his own he thought was too sentimental.) What Jones did was struggle clear of the treacly Disneyesque. (*Feed the Kitty*—treacly? No. Though it does offer a moment when audiences have been known to weep.) The great Jones films are neither sentimental nor vio-

Termite Terrace

lent, though their care for their characters could lead you to think the former while their sheer speed nudges you to the latter. *Bully for Bugs*—sentimental? Nonsense. Violent? Also nonsense, despite everything its script inflicts on a bull we surely never think is real.

A bull we never think is real—that's a tricky concept. For if we don't think of a bull the cartoon gets trivial, whereas thinking of a beast in pain expels us from the cartoon world. But that is not a beast, therefore not in pain; it's a wondrous arrangement of lines and color and movement. That's something true of all animation, and it's remarkable how much oftener the question comes up *chez* Jones than, say, *chez* Avery. Jones differs from Avery in working somewhere close to the mysterious zone where we viewers connect pen-and-ink artifice with the world we inhabit. He'd not claim ownership there, perhaps not even understanding. Still, no other animator seems to have worked in that domain with so much confidence.

In 1942, aged 30, he directed a cartoon which (he says) was "the first Chuck Jones," that is, the first film to bear what could later be recognized as his unmistakable imprint. That was *The Dover Boys,* a wondrous romp with Tom, Dick and Larry, three jolly chaps enrolled at Pimento University ("Good ole P.U.") and chastely enamored, all three, of the steadfast Dora Standpipe. The date, judging by the one auto we get to see, is oh, about 1910, so Tom, Dick and Larry get around by pedaling (one tandem, one penny-farthing, one trike). How Dora gets around is less clear. Her gown touches the ground and she seems to have no feet, but she's a dynamic wonder as she glides down stairs and wobbles like a bowling pin at each landing. Her resemblance to a bowling

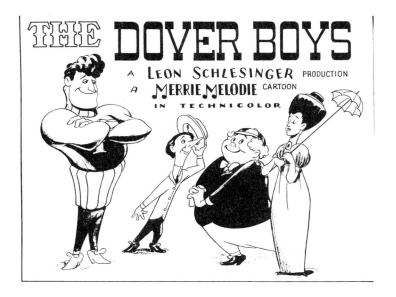

pin doesn't deter a dire fellow named Dan Backslide, who hangs out in pool-halls and, yes, covets chaste Dora. Pool-halls, we know about those; in one wonderful shot our three heroes and Dora glide by such a place on bikes, each averting a horrified gaze. Then—well, you have to see it. There's not a false move, a false moment. Movement is crisp, and stylized in a way that would be seeming normal perhaps twenty years later.[9] And, weirdest of all the weird details in *The Dover Boys*, a queer little bald bearded fellow in a swimsuit who has more than once caught our attention by intermittent hops across

9. In his memoir *Talking Animals and Other People* (1986), the great animator Shamus Culhane has John Hubley saying (p. 240) that *The Dover Boys* was a prime inspiration for the UPA cartoons of the 1950s, fabled for their "style."

Termite Terrace

the bottom of the screen (one-two-three-**HOP!**) turns out to
be the final winner of Dora Standpipe's heart as he and she
hop away into a satisfyingly clichéd sunset. (Jones's Minah
Bird, of whom more later, had that Hop mannerism too; and
you'll recall Jones recalling a long-ago time when animators
could get a laugh just by making a walking figure suddenly
Hop. He's a stubborn clinger, is Jones, to what he perceives
as validated conventions.)

A strange film, *The Dover Boys,* a clean break with Dis-
neyfication and perfectly self-contained as few Warner cartoons could think of being back in '42. That contentment in
being self-contained is one of its Chuck Jones trademarks. So
is its restriction of Animation's whole repertoire to a few formulaic devices. You don't lose when you restrict, no, you
gain. That's true of all Art, and a maxim Animation was too
long a time validating. Out in Burbank the Disney folk were
never sure that there was any limit between what they were
doing and utter hang-it-all Realism. (T. S. Eliot, whom they
didn't read, had supplied a theme for pondering a decade
previously. What had killed off a theater the glory of which
was Shakespeare, had been, Eliot postulated, its limitless ap-
petite for Realism.)

Now about the Minah Bird. It first turns up as early as
1939, in a film called *Little Lion Hunter.* It's still present in
several successors, till as late as 1950 *(Caveman Inki).* In each
film Inki, a little black fellow with a spear, seems to be the
only human inhabitant of a jungle so stylized its white hills
resemble molars. Armed solely with a spear, he hunts such
critters as a parrot, a giraffe, a butterfly. (A spear, for a butterfly! Much isn't adding up.) Through Inki's universe there
leaps, occasionally, the Minah Bird. It's black, and intent on
nobody knows what, and it has that mannerism of hopping

on every third step, guided by the rhythm of Mendelssohn's *Fingal's Cave* overture. Every time it appears, normal causation is suspended; but if you think it's Inki's good angel you're deceived, since Inki does tend to benefit but never wholly. Thus at the end of *Inki and the Minah Bird* (1943) the lion is chasing Inki into the sunset, but the Minah Bird has acquired the lion's false teeth, and what danger a toothless lion is likely to be is something on which we may speculate. (That lion, by the way, is a wonder, animated by Shamus Culhane, the same who had marched Disney's Seven Dwarfs singing "Heigh Ho!" Some eight years before Inki, Culhane attended classes taught by the same teacher Jones is proud to credit, Don Graham. And at the zoo to which Graham took the class once a month, Culhane recalls being captivated by "a mangy-looking lion," said to have once been the model for the MGM titles, but by then "the sorriest King of Beasts I ever saw."[10] Drawings he made there supplied "the best poses" for Inki's lion. And Chuck Jones was especially pleased because a lion's hind legs, for once, got animated correctly.)

Jones claims not to understand his Minah Bird films. He also claims that they drove Walt Disney to distraction. "Make something as funny as that," Walt ordered his staff, and nobody could because nobody could grasp the formula. Nor could Jones, though he made at least five of them. That such strange enigmatic things ever achieved release is a mark of the Schlesinger studio in those days. Perhaps Leon's yacht explains something. "He was a very vulgar, peculiar, naive, lovely man," Jones once recalled, and that cascade of adjectives signals something unusual. "He once bought a yacht

10. See *Talking Animals and Other People,* pp. 134 and 246–51.

from Richard Arlen and called it the 'Merrie Melodie,' with a
little dinghy on the back that he called 'Looney Tunes.' One
day I said, 'Mr. Schlesinger, when are you going to take us
out on your yacht?' And he replied, 'I don't want any poor
people on my boat.' But, of course, he was the reason we
were poor."[11] And their poverty helps explain what we'd best
be grateful for now, Leon's scant attention to their doings on
the Terrace.

11. Steve Schneider, *That's All Folks!* (1988), p. 38.

J ack and Harry, the take-charge Warner brothers, were notorious for interfering with anything they thought they understood. Their malaise pertained to the profit margin on features, which tended to be thin and was easily violated by directors whose pretensions to "artistry" kept them fussing with angles and retakes while the clock ticked. Two minutes and a half of usable footage each day was a feature director's normal quota. Back before he bolted Warners for MGM (and *The Wizard of Oz*), Mervyn LeRoy was valued for routinely doubling that.

Resources were dispensed as through an eye-dropper. The director of *Emile Zola* wanted a crowd of 400. Allotted just 200, he lowered the lighting to "rainy day" level and deployed 400 umbrellas, only half of which had people under them. The director of *The Private Lives of Elizabeth and Essex* was ordered not to let any sets be dismantled since their reuse in the upcoming *Sea Hawk* would "save a fortune."

Jack Warner, whom *Fortune* in 1937 called "a jocose penny-watcher,"[1] saw to it that Warner Bros. avoided co-starred features because those would mean paying two stars. In the pre-war decade when the house style was established, the Warners tended to concentrate on pictures one male actor—Paul Muni, Jimmy Cagney—could dominate. They preferred, too, darkness and fog, because sets you couldn't see didn't need constructing. An in-house memo of 1937—not from a Warner but in the Warner spirit—instructs a director not to "pump too much fog into the foreground in gusts." Artistic criteria? Fiscal? Uncertain. Around the same time, Jack Warner's attention was being mesmerized by the tint of Errol Flynn's mustache: "The mustache certainly looks good. I am sure that the mustache is the thing for this picture." (That was *Lives of a Bengal Lancer*.)

Mustaches after all came cheap, and "cut-rate dreaming" was the *Fortune* writer's phrase for the whole operation. He cited Harry Warner: "Listen, a picture, all it is is an expensive dream. Well, it's just as easy to dream for $700,000 as for $1,500,000."[2] (Meanwhile, over at the Disney dream-factory, *Snow White and the Seven Dwarfs* was running up a tab—for a venture in animation!—of more than the million-and-a-half that gave Harry Warner shudders at night.)

---

1. Someone less tactful once said Jack's suits had rubber pockets so he could steal soup.

2. In 1937 dollars, of course. For an early-90s equivalent try multiplying by about 10. And that's just to adjust for inflation. Today's overhead—color, special effects, union scale boosts—costs easily another fivefold. So in the 1990s animated features were enjoying a comeback after decades of eclipse. However labor-intensive, they were actually cheaper to make than damn-the-budget live action.

Life in a Comma-Factory

Warners, by the early 1940s, owned 17,000 movie-houses
in 7,500 towns, a total of 10,500,000 paying seats. Keep fill-
ing those seats, was the word that went to directors. And
every fortnight, preferably oftener, went the word to Termite
Terrace, We need one snappy new cartoon.

Yet, whatever horror stories linger in veterans' memories,
Termite Terrace, unlike any other Warner Bros. division, ran
with a singular minimum of interference. So complex was its
operation, you might have expected an accountant's face at
every transom. But no. And why not?

For one thing, the Warners didn't own the place till as late
as 1944. They simply bought its product from Leon Schlesinger Productions. And after they took over, and installed
Eddie Selzer as boss, though Eddie was a bore and a nuisance
the Brothers seemingly weren't. Jack Warner's recorded in-
terferences, though catastrophic, were but two: when he
closed the studio briefly in 1953, then for good in 1963.
Beyond that, the indifference does seem out of character. But
look, the cartoon division wasn't important. That may well
be an explanation.

For examine something else that's unimportant. I press a key.
A comma appears on my computer screen. Now how did that
happen?

Even at its simplest—on an IBM desktop machine—the
sequence is unbelievably intricate. That key closes its unique
combination of circuits. Next, a keyboard microchip, prod-
ded to do something, wakes up. Checking the active circuits
against a list, it emits a "Scan Code"—*comma!* The code goes
to an Interrupt Service Routine, which is contained in a De-
vice Driver, which has seven subsections you don't want to
hear about, all essential to handling that tiny Scan Code. Like

phone girls and file clerks guarding an Executive Producer, they cater to the whims of the Boss Microchip, the Central Processing Unit. It's possible, for instance, that the CPU may have other things on its mind which had better not be violated. So, clear its desk! And fourteen separate items, which may or may not be important (but you never know), get squirreled to safety by a head flunky, just to free high-level attention for the incoming comma. And now (music up!) the Scan Code can be ceremoniously placed in a sacred area called the Data Buffer. Only after that does the CPU get its fourteen items back so it can go on with its deliberations if it has any. What happens next depends on whether, when I pushed that key, I was running a program or just doodling. If a program, well, it's still more complicated. . . . But the Data Buffer is retentive, and eventually (we're counting in milliseconds) a little comma does emerge from its entrails to show up on the screen, while thousands cheer.

The sequencing of events at Termite Terrace, to generate a cartoon every ten to fourteen days, was at least as convoluted as that. The point of the parallel is that no one cares how a comma hits the screen so long as it gets there. Fast. And no one at Warners seems to have cared, either, how a cartoon got to 17,000 screens, so long as it reached them on schedule. Life at Termite Terrace was, blessedly, Life in a Comma-Factory. The product? Merely a punctuation mark, just before the two-reeler that came just before the feature. And the moral is, What Freedom!

By about 1949, the beginning of the Chuck Jones Golden Era, several economies had long been installed. Each, in the Warner spirit, ought to have been a hobble. At Termite Terrace each was a liberation.

First, how much footage? Cartoons ran about 7 minutes.

At 420 seconds, that's 10,080 frames, or 5,040 drawings when we shoot each of them twice. A lot of drawings. Even at starvation wages, a lot of money: say $30,000 per Looney Tune: say three-quarters of a million bucks annually, plus change.

That's about the cost of one middling 90-minute feature; and for about twice the delivered footage per year! Foot for foot, Termite Terrace might seem a bargain.

Still, it's features, not cartoons, that draw the crowds. Cartoons being trivial, something seemed out of balance. Seven minutes per product: might exhibitors stand for less? It turned out they'd regard five minutes as short weight. The compromise was six; six minutes plus or minus a grotesquely specified two-thirds of a second. Standardization #1: *Scale as fixed as the size of a window at Chartres.*

Next, we've got to get this place organized. Every two weeks, that's twenty-six a year; three directors can handle that, each responsible for about ten films. From conception to delivery, a cartoon might take twelve months or more. So a director at any time had ten or more going at once, the newest just being talked out, the oldest acquiring its sound track, perhaps eight others in stages of gestation. Thus, Standardization #2: *The picture belongs to the director.*

That system was firmly in place by 1944, when the Warners bought Schlesinger out. By 1947 the three directors were Isadore (Friz) Freleng, Charles Martin (Chuck) Jones, Robert (Bob) McKimson. And the control of each, over each project credited to him, was, finally, absolute. Termite Terrace being the only shop where so rigid a system was installed to meet so exacting a schedule, the Warner Bros. cartoon division was likely the only place in all of cinedom to which the *auteur* theory can be rigidly applied.

Auteur is what the French call an author, a creator; and *auteur* theory was something film historian Andrew Sarris began promoting about 1968, to celebrate, as his gadfly Thomas Schatz puts it, "the director as the sole purveyor of Film Art in an industry overrun with hacks and profitmongers." Schatz calls that "adolescent romanticism"; his *The Genius of the System* (1988) is persuasive about hacks and profitmongers not sabotaging good films, but imposing the limits that made good films possible. For art is largely an affair of limits. When the Medici asked for a panel of certain dimensions to adorn, as it were, their summer cottage, that was when they got Botticelli's *Venus.*

Schatz, though, nowhere mentions the cartoon operations maintained by the studio systems he surveys: a pity, since the reason we have such a book as Steve Schneider's *That's All Folks!* (subtitled, *The Art of Warner Bros. Animation*) is that the Warner system, albeit by inadvertence, guaranteed a niche where miracles could happen: where "Art," an overused word, is fitfully applicable.

And the time has come to demystify the Termite Terrace usage of "Director." The DeMille image—bawling through a megaphone at actors—is inapplicable; there was no Bugs Bunny to bawl at, save as numerous pencils created him at the rate of twelve drawings per second (every frame shot twice, remember?) Over at Disney, to say that Art Babbitt supervised one of *Fantasia*'s highest points, the Chinese Mushroom Dance, or that Shamus Culhane marched the Seven Dwarfs off, Heigh Ho, is to say we don't know what we're saying, since (as Jones remarks) the head animator of a Disney sequence worked with a sequence director, who in turn had the privilege of consulting the film director, who might consult

Walt. Also, Walt might just drop in. So we can't tell when or how often Walt may have been involved. Walt, a mediocre animator but a storyman of genius, had the last word on every detail and would order things redone from scratch. At Warners they didn't enjoy the luxury of redoing. Just get it the way it's going to be, the first time round.

Hence the Director's necessary iron control. Briefly: he confabbed with the storymen, he worked with the soundmen; he knew the strengths of his key Animators; he knew their In-betweeners. He drew "Model Sheets" to help numerous hands keep his characters unified. (Jones's Bugs isn't Freleng's Bugs.) And his crucial role came down to (1) making 300 or up to 500 key drawings to guide the Animators; (2) making frame-by-frame plans called Exposure Sheets that would bring the thing out exactly on the last second (360 seconds, that's 4,320 drawn frames, give or take a half-dozen.) With ten or twelve projects under way on any morning, the director might be shown one of up to 50,000 drawings, by some underling in a jam. Unflappable, he'd recognize its place in which sequence of which film. Such talent was rare, the knack for those key drawings rarer still, command of the Exposure Sheets likely rarest of all. Great as the best Warner Animators were, it's no wonder so few became Directors.

Chuck Jones tended to make more key drawings than the other directors. They show how a sequence of movement is to begin and end. He's explicit about their role. The Animator wasn't to trace them. The Animator was to use them as guides, defining a flurry of drawings he could feel happy with. "Ken Harris will change everything. He'll use an idea, but the action will flow through and go beyond it. Or he may forget it completely. But his animation will indicate what I had in mind." One facet of directing is prodding the very best out of such a rare talent as Harris's.

(And the In-betweeners? A hack In-betweener, as the art had evolved by the era we're speaking of, might as well be computerized—something that's still being worked on—but a good one, moving toward Animator status, understood how between key frames different parts of a creature shift different weights at different velocities. As the foot comes to rest, the body still lurches forward. Great animators insist that there is no such thing as an exact in-between, equidistant between extremes. So cherish your In-betweeners, who generate possibly 80 percent of the frames that end up, inked and painted, on-screen.)

The Animators also kept a wary eye on the director's other principal offering, the Exposure Sheet. It's a printed strip of sturdy paper, about nine inches wide by twenty long, ruled with a horizontal line for every frame, plus emphatic lines for feet of film, seconds of time. Every drawing we're going to generate gets accounted for there, every footstep, drumbeat, syllable of dialogue. No live-action *auteur* could have dreamed of such command. And each sheet takes care of 6 feet. So 540 feet of film—6 minutes—means 90 of those sheets, a thickish stack.

Bugs Bunny is walking 12 paces per foot (at 12 drawn frames per foot, that's a second per pace). Down the left-hand column, "Action," an X at every 12th line means a foot touching ground; key drawings will guide the Animator there. And Bugs is saying (what else?) "What's up, Doc?" In the next column ("Dialog"), at frame 8, the "Wh" commences (his mouth starts to open); by frame 16 his mouth is wide open on the "ah"; by frame 22 it's closed on the "ts." That kind of thing is plotted on the Exposure Sheet for every syllable of dialogue; the mouth-closing "c" that ends "Doc" coincides with frame 52 (drawing 26). The rule is that sound can escape the mouth only on vowels, consonants determining the beginning and finish of the vowel sound. On *M, F, P,* the mouth closes. On *T, N, L,* the tongue goes up against the roof of the mouth. Such are the instants the director needs to locate for the Animator, so the timing of dialogue will flow aright. Between such key points, a competent Animator is on his own. At Warners they had some *very* competent Animators.

Jones can tell, he says, if timing is off by one frame. That's less than an eyeblink. Prescriptions could be unbelievably precise. When the Coyote dropped off the cliff, as he did repeatedly, it would take, says Jones, "Eighteen frames for him to fall into the distance and disappear, then fourteen frames later he would hit. It seemed to me that thirteen frames didn't work in terms of humor, and neither did fifteen frames. Fourteen frames got a laugh." And from the Exposure Sheet all hands—Animators, In-betweeners, Sound Crew—knew exactly what was required.

But there's more. In addition to a wide rightmost block headed "Camera Instructions," where you'd specify, say, panning the next forty frames across a wide background, the Exposure Sheet has six more numbered columns. Those are for any special high-jinks with cels. Because if Elmer Fudd holds still and just moves his lips to say "Wabbit season," the main Elmer-cell, to save a lot of redrawing, can just be overlaid with a sequence of mouth-cels. You might find yourself repeating that principle for several layers, trusting someone in Ink-and-Paint to remember that colors change when they're perceived down through overlaid cels. To keep Elmer's red jacket Elmer-red beneath three cels meant calling for a richer red with a special number.

Life in a Comma-Factory

And let's attend anew to one phrase: "to save a lot of re-drawing." If that began as a concession to the cash-register, it soon became a principle of art. Recall Gertie the Dinosaur, of pre-cel days, when endless retracing made everything shimmer and wobble. But cels let us think of shimmer and wobble as special effects. Special too is the non-wobbling rigidity of drawings simply reused. So as animation evolved post-cel, just what changes *now* becomes what matters, to offset what—for two seconds (eternity!)—isn't changing. That gets emphasis Animators can get in no other way: think of Elmer's obsessed rigidity as he listens for wabbits. Maybe eyes blink (overlaid cels); maybe they don't. Selective redrawing became, especially at Warners, one of animation's subtlest modes of expression. What the Termite Terrace zanies found in it resembles Milton's discovery, circa 1660, of the range of effects blank verse on a printed page could extract from a mid-line pause: Line visible, stable; Pause audible, fluctuant.

What that does is throw emphasis back on the key drawings: the moments of stasis, of expressive posture, which might even stay frozen for several frames. At Disney the emphasis was on fluent movement; at Warners, the prolific Friz Freleng's habit tended that way too. It was during stretches of dialogue that Disney's custom was to introduce punctuating pauses, where they can be subtly irritating simply because they're meaningless. But Chuck Jones cherished the summarizing key pose, and his Exposure Sheets were apt to instruct that it be held: held an exact number of frames. And of such was his kingdom of heaven.

Generally, as a cost-saver, the largest number of characters visible in one shot was two.[3] Thus in the Hunting Trilogy of 1951–53 (*Rabbit Fire; Rabbit Seasoning; Duck! Rabbit! Duck!*), though each film revolved around three characters—Elmer Fudd, mighty hunter; Bugs Bunny, cool evader; Daffy Duck, hysterical victim—the economical strategy was to establish their relationship, then resort to "one-shots" and "two-shots." And the two-shots could economize too, by just "looking at one of the characters" without troubling to animate him. Thus, "Daffy would say, 'Oh, no you don't,' and Bugs would just stand there waiting. Because that is what he would do anyway." Chuck Jones guesses that in a given picture, perhaps 60 percent of the shots use just one character. "We soon learned that it was not just to cut down on the number of separately animated cels, but to emphasize the power of a strongly-drawn non-talker as a foil for the voluble. It became what I call Motivated Camera. Having established the rhythm of the relationship between two characters, I could go to one for something to say, go to the other for the reaction. We learned to do it pretty well." Indeed they did. Something from the Hunting Trilogy tends to show up on most lists of Warner cartoon highlights.

An economic necessity, true; but there's no denying how, here as so often, necessity "resulted in far better picture-making."

And for another interesting reason: "It also resulted in our cutting all the fat out of our dialogue. I mean, if you have something to say, say it. You know."

---

3. By contrast, there are scenes in *Snow White* where as many as thirty animals are all differently busied. But cost wasn't governing such scenes.

And to show that I knew, I volunteered, "Get the meaning across and then stop."[4]

And Jones, good liberal that he is, responded with "Woodrow Wilson, I think it was, who said, If you're shooting, do not use a shotgun, use a rifle with a single bullet; likewise when you're writing." That's the one time I've heard an ex-president of Princeton cited as a monitor of verbal style.

One can hardly overestimate the extent to which the Warner Cartoon Style stemmed from the need to minimize costs. "If I had suggested doing *101 Dalmatians* everyone would have thought I was crazy. Even a dog named Spot, with one spot, would have been out of the question. What costs in animation isn't colorful and detailed backgrounds; those are its cheapest elements, because a short with maybe 65 backgrounds will still need 5,000 drawings. It's the details in those drawings that cost. When Disney made *101 Dalmatians,* the animators didn't animate dalmatians, they animated white dogs. Somebody else came along and put the spots on. O. Henry said that the most exacting (make that 'exasperating') job in the world was that of foreman to a gang of invisible weavers. I'm not so sure."

And they kept the spots consistent on each dog?

"No, they animated just eight different dogs. That was the first time they used a computer, for the few scenes when you see the whole pack of puppies at once. It decided how to randomize eight dogs repeatedly so that 101 of them running at you would look like 101 dogs rather than a dozen-plus sets of eight."

4.   From Ezra Pound's *Cantos,* where the sense is attributed to Confucius.

Limited animation

Full animation

Ramifications of the need to economize are not, alas, infallibly benign. Saturday morning television would bring about what the film critic Leonard Maltin calls the Muzak of animation.[5] Chuck Jones once summed up what *he* calls it in one

5. *Film Comment,* January–February 1975, p. 77.

Life in a Comma-Factory

ELMER   BUGS   DAFFY   PEPE

savage drawing. He also adduces what Groucho Marx called TV: "The chewing-gum of the eye." But defenders have a cushion-word, "limited," and Limited Animation even gets touted as an artistic discovery, perhaps because UPA's stylizations of the '50s, partly derived from *The Dover Boys,* resembled it just enough to bemuse the hasty.

Limited Animation stemmed from the fix Bill Hanna and Joe Barbera, creators of the Tom and Jerry duo, found themselves in when their twenty-year connection with the MGM cartoon department was terminated with a phone call in 1957. That was when all the studios were getting out of animation: too much expense, too little return. (Newsreels were out; so were shorts, not to mention cartoons; the norm was becoming a Continuous Performance of maybe a single feature or maybe two.) Hanna and Barbera moved to TV, where they discovered that their MGM quota, 50 minutes of film a year,[6] had jumped up to over an hour a week. You can see what that dictates: as few different drawings per film as possi-

6. That means, seven cartoons a year, each seven minutes. "Rich kids," comments C. J.

Life in a Comma-Factory

RUN ATTITUDES -
DIFFERENT CHAR

PORKY · FOGHORN · HENERY · TWEETY

ble, which means, Maltin notes, that "all action takes place on the same plane"—no camera movement in and out, so a walk can just be the same few frames woodenly repeated. Also, no "tedious detail"; which means, says Maltin, that "wriggling an eyebrow would probably throw off the budget for an entire series." And every character walks like every other character, so out the window goes the very essence of Character Animation, which (remember?) defines a character by ways of moving.

"They blink when someone's talking," says Chuck Jones. "That's big stuff. To establish that the character is alive. What you have is two eye drawings, one closed, one open. And you leave the closed one on for eighteen frames." (There an expert eye has spotted the convention—a three-quarters-of-a-second blink.) "Or you have a whole bunch of people running, and you cut at the waist so you don't have to move the legs. And nobody moves off into the background or comes forward, because that takes a lot of drawings. Everything parallel to the camera, the same eight drawings over and over."

SYLVESTER   COYOTE

That leads him to a richer theme: "We never, in all the years I was at Warners, repeated the same run for Bugs or for Daffy or any other character. Never. I always felt there was something different in the character's mind. So the animators had the pleasure of trying out a lot of runs. They knew there is a lot of difference between running when you're being chased and running when you are chasing. And there's also a lot of difference, as in the Pepé Le Pew pictures, between running out of desperation, as his paramour is doing, or running out of joy, as he is doing. He didn't know what desperation was."

Pepé's most joyous run is modeled on the pronk, a word devised in South Africa a century ago to denote the springbok's vertical leaps. (It's from the Dutch *pronken,* to strut.) In Chapter 8 of their *Fearful Symmetry: Is God a Geometer?* Ian Stewart and Martin Golubitsky list pronking, "all four legs moved at the same time," as the least frequent of the eight main quadupedal gaits. It's uncommon, they remark, outside of cartoons (as they illustrate with a *Garfield* panel), though "sometimes seen in fast-moving deer." The Pepé pronk is a sequence of ecstatic vertical leaps, all four feet leaving the

ground at once, forward movement perhaps half of vertical, eyes wide, tongue lolling, the whole danced to a dream-tempo metronome that's wholly decoupled from the panic of any springbok. It's contemplative, and what its contemplation postulates is leisurely future bliss, untarnished by any cynicism about Jam Tomorrow but never Jam Today. Character Animation: so much can inhere in a way of moving.

One more thing: after 1944, directors dealt with producer Eddie Selzer, who always demanded to see scripts and never grasped that there weren't any (cartoons are storyboarded, not scripted). They learned to take a 180-degree turn from any judgment of Eddie's. "Bullfights aren't funny." Hence, *Bully for Bugs,* which Jones once called "The ultimate Bugs Bunny film."[7] And skunks talking French weren't funny? *Voilà!* Pepé Le Pew (who won an Oscar, graciously accepted by Eddie). Schlesinger, Jones remarks, had seldom even the energy required to say No, whereas Selzer said little else.

Something Eddie Selzer once found especially unfunny was four or five grown men laughing out loud over a story-

---

7.   As for getting Eddie to pay for the crew's fact-finding trip to Mexico: "He didn't; and he subtracted the time from our vacation allotment."

Life in a Comma-Factory

56 board. What the hell, he wanted to know, did all this laughter have to do with the job? (His tiny eyes, Jones recalls, were "steely as half-thawed oysters." Those are eyes perceived by an animator's eye. Eyes become steel becomes oysters. The stuff of animation is metamorphosis, and its theoretician ought to have been Ovid.)

So now you've an idea of what it meant to be a cartoon director. Are you relieved not to have been one? In a quarter-century Chuck Jones, if I've counted correctly, directed 204 Warner Brothers cartoons. A handful are masterpieces of the art. Abstractly remote from what an audience will see, Directing is a difficult process from which to wring masterpieces. "I didn't do it for kids," Jones has said more than once; "I did it for myself."

He's been called the most gifted animation director who ever lived. As he likely is. But in no area has civilization ever been a one-man job. Consider (1) that he'd not have had such an opportunity save at that one studio, where every pinchpenny gesture chanced to broaden the director's scope; (2) that sheer serendipity surrounded him for a few years with an incredible constellation of talents, all eccentric, as for good animation they'd best be. Michael Maltese, writer; Maurice Noble, background designer; Ken Harris, Benny Washam, and Abe Levitow—to name only three—animators; Carl Stalling, music; Mel Blanc, voices; and more; and rarely do such frenzies converge. (When Mel Blanc died the same week as Laurence Olivier, someone asked what production God might be pondering for Heaven.)

A fistful of dice, and every throw came up boxcar.

Maltese, to start with; "writer," though he'd write no words till it came time to suggest dialogue. There was never, as

Eddie Selzer couldn't grasp, a script. There was a "storyboard," four feet by eight, that ended up holding some 150
sketches. These graphed the course of a six-minute picture.
The writer (who couldn't really draw)[8] and the director (who
really could) put them there in the course of some five weeks'
interaction. It had started from an "idea" (generally the
writer's), such as "A male rabbit singing Brünnhilde's role
against a mighty eighty-piece symphony orchestra." (That
one led to a masterpiece: *What's Opera, Doc?*)

The mind of Maltese teemed with swift incongruities. The
day he rode a wobbly elevator, his instant response was
"Good to the Last Drop." Unlike Tedd Pierce, his predecessor on the Jones Team, Maltese had rather a gag-man's talents than a narrative architect's; compare Pierce's *The Dover
Boys,* with its stress on an overarching plot, with any Maltese
Road Runner, essentially a sequence of perhaps six major gags.

The storyboard's centrality, by the way, underlies a frequent Jones dictum: that any cartoon you can follow by ear
without looking is merely "illustrated radio." Real animation
holds you even with the sound turned off. Its kind of story,
whether plot or gag-train, had to be planned via sketches—
"dealing with graphics, not adjectives, from the start"—and
the process seemed to take almost a week per minute.[9]

But five weeks' work might not lead anywhere interesting. To head off that danger, a "Jam Session" would be con-
vened after week one. It included all three directors, their
three writers, others, and the ground rule was that no one
might say "no." Impart further spin to the ball, or else stay

8. Though Maltese about 1938 did time as an in-betweener.

9. Hereabouts, I find among my notes, in C. J.'s hand, "O. Henry once defined a character as about the size of a real estate agent. Now *there* is a provoca-
tive stage direction."

Life in a Comma-Factory

quiet. Within a half hour, much silence might suggest that the "idea" just wasn't working. Otherwise, two hours of creative input: from writers, and from directors (Freleng, McKimson) who knew that their next Jam Session would be profiting by input from Mike Maltese and Chuck Jones, just as Chuck and Mike would expect—and receive—wholehearted support from Freleng, Foster and Pierce.

(Hard to keep all these balls aloft; you're staying aware, yes, that on any day each director, each writer, was at some stage or other of maybe a dozen projects? How they concentrated on a Jam Session defies imagining.)

Next, Maurice Noble, Background Designer; and why do we need such a Designer? Well, while everyone else is minding masses of detail on a fractions-of-a-second scale, somebody has to be thinking of what the audience will *see:* a six-minute whole punctuated by notable details. The total look of the picture is what will contain their attention. This one is a *murky* film; this one is *crisp;* the audience won't think that way, but that's what they'll respond to. Noble, who'd done backgrounds for Disney's *Snow White* and parts of *Fantasia,* notably the Mushroom Dance, was to work with Chuck Jones for twenty years. His responsibility was for overall look and feel.

At Warners he didn't paint backgrounds, but his designs guided the people who did. Jones has described how their collaboration worked. "What I did was draft a very rough plan, just to show the layout man what I wanted. If I put in a doorway, all I wanted was room for the character to exit; I didn't care what the doorway looked like. Maurice would take my layouts—let's say there'd be ten layouts for the scene—and make a sort of *mise-en-scène* that defines the limits of the character action. He'd find the layout that goes the furthest to the right, the one that goes the furthest to the left, the deepest one, the closest one, and generally plan where most of the action would have to fall. He'd take all these separate layouts and put them all in one drawing, and then design the background around it. He'd also take into consideration what was happening in the story—which very few background men ever do. Generally speaking, the foreground characters were all mine, but Maurice would also often design background characters which were visually very strong, like those Baroque-looking French bystanders in the later Pepé Le Pew cartoons."[10]

Noble had a lot to do with specifying colors, often against the resistance of the ink-and-paint crew. ("Do you really want this red next to this red?" "Yes." And, Noble likes to recall, "Chuck would back me up.") For the ballet sequence in *What's Opera, Doc?* he moved areas of flesh tint into the backgrounds, to make up for the unfleshly grayness of the prima ballerina, played by Bugs Bunny in drag. He also made sure that in the opening frames the shadow Siegfried/Fudd cast on a mountain's face would uncannily recall the "Chernabog" Devil in *Fantasia* (a prime feat of animation, by Disney's Bill Tytla, to which Termite Terracers more than once alluded). And for *Duck Dodgers in the 24½ Century* he devised a spaceport so realistic, post-Apollo, it's hard to believe it dates from 1953, when Cape Kennedy hadn't been dreamt of. "Chuck would back me up" because Chuck held that a director who attempted his own designs, like the lawyer who pled his own case, had a fool for a client. And Chuck would also judge, in 1975, that of the people he'd ever worked with Maurice Noble was probably the most influential.

10. Interview in *Film Comment*, January–February 1975, pp. 28–9.

Mel Blanc, finally: "Voice Characterizations," as the credits always said. And here was someone whose contribution, delivered in real time, on a live mike, could not be fiddled with the way you might fiddle with an in-between drawing. Mel might do it over and over, but what was finally used wasn't something you'd achieved by editing, but something Mel had *done*. (Not that technicians hadn't altered pace and pitch electronically while Mel did Porky or Tweety.) Mel could be Bugs one moment and Elmer Fudd the next; but the way it was really achieved, he'd record the Elmer Fudd speeches while Chuck Jones fed him the Daffy Duck outrages, then the Bugs dismissals while Chuck fed him what Daffy had been outraged by, and so on and on. And, Chuck Jones recalls, they'd stop doing that whenever Mel Blanc had recorded the same speech three times. (Thereafter, it's implied, live performers tend to deteriorate into rote.) But if Chuck wasn't happy with any of the first three recordings he'd sometimes suggest to Mel that he, Chuck, had perhaps botched his feeder-speech, so might they try it again?

And that is, more or less, how it was done: how the miracles were achieved, right through the Golden Age: from the mid-'40s through the mid-'60s.

We've been describing a team that had come together by about 1949; a convenient date since it happens to be the year of the first Road Runner film, *Fast and Furry-ous*. But by then, good lord, Chuck Jones, 37, had been Supervising, as they once called Directing, since March 1938, when he was a mere 25. That was when Frank Tashlin had just left Warners, and young Chuck, who'd been animating for Tex Avery, became his emergency replacement. How scarce experienced talent must have been! Walt Disney had brought a bunch of "experienced" youngsters westward by about 1925, the year his

Kansas friends Harman and Ising joined him in Los Angeles. And Jones's colleague Friz Freleng, for heaven's sake, born 1906, thus a mere six years Jones's senior, had been one of Disney's Kansas City migrants; which means that by the late '30s, when Leon Schlesinger was being hard-put to get a staff together after Harman and Ising left him, the people who'd been around animation long enough to know what they were doing, yet weren't so firmly established as no longer to be for hire, were all of them still conspicuously young. A 25-year-old *director,* name of, ah, Jones? To which an answer would be, O.K., find us someone more plausible. It was very much a young person's game. If, by today's standards, work often got crudely done, still the right young person, under pressure, might learn the Whole Art fast. And that diagrams the story of Chuck Jones.

So "I had to learn the language, and so did my animators. We had classes—for years we had at least two classes per week, at night. And we were working a five-and-a-half day week, about fifty-six hours a week."[11]

And, about *Good Night Elmer* (1940), "The story was just a tiny thing: a man attempting to put out a little candle. How can you make an entire story about that? Is it possible? That's what I wanted to know. I wouldn't say it was a particularly successful picture; but it was crucial in terms of what came afterward." The Beck-Friedwald entry on that film ends on a note of unaccustomed anguish: "One of the most irritating cartoons ever made. There was no reason to animate this, everything in this cartoon could have been easily filmed in live action. Chuck Jones's early super-slow timing at its most

---

11. Again, *Film Comment,* January–February 1975, p. 22. This whole interview is a prime source.

brutal (hard to believe that this man would later make the super-speed Road Runner cartoons). And Elmer is so stupid it's painful!" *Good Night Elmer* is not a film I've seen; I'm simply reporting. But I'll draw attention to Jones's "Is it possible?" and the perhaps implied answer, No, not with the resources the director could bring to it at 28. We've likewise alluded to his long Disneyfied period. Well, think of that as more learning. And reflect that the breakthrough *Dover Boys* was achieved when he was just 30. (And by then he'd been directing for fully four years: had directed all of forty films. That amounts to some four-plus hours of screen time, the Director held accountable for every one of a dozen drawings per second. That in turn implies a *lot* of learning.)

One principle he learned is that believability is more important than realism; also that one thing that helps the animator achieve believability is a sense of what his characters weigh. Yes, *weigh*. It's clear from his manner of moving that the bull in *Bully for Bugs* (1953) is enormously heavy. Likewise, it's evident that when Willis O'Brien, the puppet-master of the original *King Kong* (1933), moved his furry eighteen-inch tabletop ape, he was guided by a very clear sense of how much sheer bulk the muscles of the "real" or fifty-foot Kong would be wielding. And it's equally evident that the special-effects gang on the disastrous Dino di Laurentiis remake (1976) didn't know how to keep us from detecting the sequences that were shot with a man in an ape-suit. And how do we spot them? Well, no one thought to tell the actor to keep his head and shoulders level as he walked. The way he bobs, we know at once we're looking not at multiple tons but at a routine Hollywood beach-bum.

Weight and how we assess it: that's one of Chuck Jones's most eloquent topics. Some of its ramifications are far from

obvious: "A cat," for instance, "is built light, but walks
heavy." That means, the cat's spine stays a steady distance
from the ground, which is what people who say a cat
"slinks" are really reporting. A dog even twice the size of the
average full-grown cat will likely have a bouncier gait. One
wonderful Jones cartoon called *No Barking* (1954) is based on
a careful contrast of such mannerisms. A puppy named Frisky
bounds about, full of himself, as though nearly weightless; an
alley-cat named Claude is driven half mad every time such
bouncing and barking impinges on his own weighty lan-
guor. Claude will never be convinced that he's not the target
of malevolent persecution, or that Frisky is, by and large, un-
concerned about feline presence. What is making Claude's
life unliveable, and will ultimately send him out of animation's universe, clutching in panic to the underside of a trans-
continental jet, is both abstract and profound: not alien hos-
tility but an alien *rhythm*. In one memorable sequence Claude
is stealthily approaching a treetop nest, when a bark from
Frisky sends him hurtling skyward past the nest and its resident, none other than Friz Freleng's Tweety in a two-second
cameo appearance: "I tawt I taw a puddy tat." True. Frisky's
rhythm in the universe of Claude *is* cause for alarm, though
not for Tweety but for Claude.

No Barking illustrates something else Jones often comments on, the central importance of teamwork in a successful
animation venture. As Beck and Friedwald remark, that film
is devoid of human characters to supply framing dialogue; in
fact, the seven words we've just quoted are exactly all the
words Mel Blanc got to voice in the entire film. So absolutely
everything has to be communicated via styles of movement;
and "Jones relies exclusively on the studio's great animator,
Ken Harris, to do the whole cartoon." That was possible be-

cause Jones and Harris had spent years negotiating a sense of one another's habits and conventions.

"The team thing is very important," Jones told the *Film Comment* interviewers.[12] "It gets to the point where you can snap your fingers, or make a single drawing to convey your idea. Whenever a new animator came to work for me, he was in trouble for a while, because on my exposure sheets, I would put down a notation like 'BAL'—which was 'balance'—or 'ANT'—'anticipate.' And all my animators had to know exactly what they meant." And what did they mean? Well, ANT was "an anticipation before the actual motion," while BAL "might mean that I'd want a particular character solid on his feet before he did something, so you'd know there was a stability to the thing, before it moved into action." It's evident how both BAL and ANT play on what we can be induced to *expect* we'll be seeing in the next few seconds. Part of our attention is now, part's in the future. Also, "When I put down a twelve-frame hold, that didn't mean thirteen frames or eleven frames, it meant twelve frames exactly. When the Coyote fell off, I knew he had to go exactly eighteen frames into the distance and then disappear for fourteen frames before he hit. A new animator would come in and he would overlap that, and it would never work." (Eighteen frames—that's *exactly* three-quarters of a second. Something beating at an eighteen-frame rate would throb seventy-five times per minute. And that's as close as cinema technology can come to the pace per minute of a "normal" adult heartbeat, which is seventy-two. Hmmmm. A hidden Law of Nature? What "works" on-screen is what corresponds to a pulse-beat?)

12. See *Film Comment,* January–February 1975, p. 23.

And the many moods of the amorous skunk Pepé Le
Pew—most of them upbeat—are conveyed by his many
gaits, notably the frisky pronk that carries him round in cir-
cles of ecstasy, all four feet leaving the ground at the same
instant. A quality almost dream-like inheres in the lift he gets.

And a twenty-five-minute Chuck Jones TV special of
1975, *Rikki-Tikki-Tavi,* adapted from a Kipling story, is note-
worthy for having presented a special problem: how to give a
mongoose some personality we can relate to while never implying that he isn't a mongoose. We may think of Bugs
Bunny or Porky Pig as, essentially, humans who happen to
look like animals. But Rikki is a mongoose, kept by a human
family in British India the way another family might keep a
cat.

What do most of us know about the mongoose? Chiefly,
that he's deadly to poisonous snakes—the cobra comes to
mind. But don't imagine he's immune to snakebite. What
saves him is sheer speed, a habit of moving much faster than
the snake. That's the kind of information that sets an animation director thinking. For what's Rikki doing when he isn't
coping with cobras? Mostly, moving, as he always does, *fast:*
zipping in and out of humans' spaces. So Jones's model sheet
offered special routines for getting Rikki off-scene and on.
The effect has been described, not inappropriately, as an art
based on the post-retinal image. You see a blur without feel-
ing sure what you saw. Yet once it's been diagrammed it's
simple enough for any competent animator to duplicate.
Jones labeled two diagrams as follows: "When Rikki enters
the scene let him fill an imaginary Rikki until his nose
reaches the proper point. Then the rest expands and the last
movement is when his whiskers pop out and vibrate." (That
means, he streaks in lean, entering that "imaginary Rikki" via
the tail, then plumps out. The process can take up to four

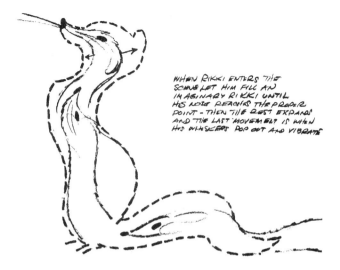

WHEN RIKKI ENTERS THE
SCENE LET HIM FILL AN
IMAGINARY RIKKI UNTIL
HIS NOSE REACHES THE PROPER
POINT - THEN THE REST EXPANDS
AND THE LAST MOVEMENT IS WHEN
HIS WHISKERS POP OUT AND VIBRATE

seconds.) And, "When Rikki leaves the scene, follow the angle of his pose. Hold tail until head is well out—then snap tail along path and out." Discussing this during a 1977 phone call, Jones drew on two interesting analogies. Envision, he said, a string of fifteen cars stopped by a red light. When the light changes, the fifteen cars won't move off *en bloc*. No, car 1 must move ahead several feet before car 2 can even start moving, likewise car 3, car 4 . . . So the string *lengthens* as it gets into motion. Or imagine that when a horse goes over a jump, the neck must move part way before it can start dragging the shoulders, then the shoulders must make some progress before they can drag the torso. Again, an effect of elongation. But, beginning at the moment the front feet hit the ground, the opposite occurs: the horse *shortens* as fluent movement comes piling up against blockage. Different parts a-move at different rates, that's a principle vital to convincing animation, also something Jones expected his staff to understand. And in-betweeners draw most of the frames where

WHEN RIKKI LEAVES THIS
SCENE FOLLOW THE ANGLE
OF HIS POSE. HOLD TAIL UNTIL
HEAD IS WELL OUT—THEN
SNAP TAIL ALONG PATH AND OUT

such things happen, one reason good in-betweening cannot be mechanized.

He's also used the cars-at-stoplight analogy to discuss the Coyote's formulaic fall. Wile E.'s torso drops away, leaving a stressed face atop a stretched-out neck. Two seconds later the contracting neck snaps the face down out of sight, leaving two long ears. When those in turn vanish we are left to ponder—oh, the reluctance of Being to succumb to Mutability.

Jones dissociates processes into parts so habitually it's doubtful if he's always aware that that's what he's doing. "The Wedge," he said one day, apropos of a time when he was serving as Vice President for Children's Programming at ABC. (And Johnny Carson once said that being a Vice President at ABC is like being dancing master at Forest Lawn.[13] The Wedge (one of Isaac Newton's six Simple Machines) was

13. A Los Angeles cemetery, if you've forgotten. It inspired Evelyn Waugh's *The Loved One.*

the theme of one film they made; and (said Jones) "When you start studying it you find there's so much there. If it wasn't for the Wedge we wouldn't have a saw. A saw is only a series of wedges." That's true, and it also says how a saw saws, by wedging bits of wood left and right so they crumble. You've spotted, surely, an Animation Director's habit of thought. What else is this piece of movement like? What can we break it down to? Decompose it to? (For that matter, what may some previous Animator have done with it? Jones credits a National Film Board of Canada production on the Wedge: "I liked it and shamelessly used it.")

It's going to end up decomposed into drawings-per-second, but like Churchill's proverbial pudding, that decomposition will go better if it's ruled by a theme. The Saw-Wedge theme I don't know about, not having seen the NFB film. The Coyote's decomposition, it is safe to say, reflects a ritual reenactment of the death of Creativity; but paradoxically, at Termite Terrace, where it never died.

his intonations after two decades) *"What part of me is the green frog?"*

Let's suggest. The Green Frog looks like nothing; but, Lord, he can perform! Frog 1: The frog as he may imagine we see him, a commonplace croaker. *Click!* Frog 2, the inner, pulsing Frog! (The Chuck Jones who would marry, successively, two talented and beautiful wives?) Or, Frog 1, a mere frog, as a videocam might pick him up: in a human context, something worth little attention. *Click!* Frog 2, a Frog transcended by animation! (And compare what Mickey did for the mere mouse.)

Who's in Charge Here?

No, neither is animation all self-portraiture, nor is it all the foregrounding of a medium, not even of a medium un-dreamed of before this century. It is, like all art, the trace of a man doing an intricate job he could not have wholly described to us. (To reach for the very top: what might Shake-speare have said of *Hamlet?* Oh, a script the company needed, with a fat part for Burbage. Or Botticelli of the *Venus?* Ah, a decoration some Medici had a whim for. Botticelli, by the way, like most painters of his era, was attended by the likes of in-betweeners: apprentices who'd attend to such trivia as robes and clouds.)

—A Thought Experiment, meant not to smuggle Chuck into exalted company; no, simply to adduce the fact that Art has normally been commissioned by folk, or by forces like the Brothers Warner, who'd had no way to guess what might later be made of it. Did Homer's tribal hearers envision a Harvard classroom? Or even the discipleship of Roman Ver-gil?

Of course not. Nor did hundreds of thousands of viewers of Jones cartoons—who'd never heard of Chuck Jones—ever imagine the "Joneses" disengaged from the "Frelengs" and the "McKimsons" for separate contemplation, let alone serious discussion. Those viewers saw a Warner Bros. car-toon when they happened to visit a movie-house that was showing one, and it was unlikely to have been for the car-toon that they'd paid that visit. In those gone times the Car-toon and the Newsreel and the Short were merely french fries that got served in a two-hour package with the feature. (Likewise, a recitation of a new chunk of the *Æneid* was something you might have put up with when your business was an audience with the Emperor Augustus.)

It's important, therefore, to glimpse both how slight and how inclusive a claim we make when we adduce other arts in other times. In most times and places what we've come to call "art" was created to satisfy some market. Also, it was brought into being according to procedures which could be articulated, taught, learnt. There were masters, and apprentices aspiring to be masters. How many people worked on the Sistine Ceiling? We think of Michelangelo; but he'd have had helpers. They were learning to do what he did, much as Inbetweeners learn to Animate and perhaps aspire to Direct.

But Renaissance painting is only a partial analogy for studio animation. The nearest full analogy for that seems to be Wagnerian opera, which requires expert set-designers, virtuosos of lighting, voice-coaches, scene-changers, costumers, nowadays experts at getting the unobtrusive microphone into the right place, even someone adept at comforting a sulky bassoon. Likewise, as we've seen, Chuck Jones's concentration on timing and expression, his complementarity with animators of the quality of Harris, Washam, and Levitow, needed further complementing by Maltese (story), Noble (layouts), Stalling (music), Blanc (voices) . . . and more and more and more, clear down to the ink-and-paint women whose deft hands made the cels the camera saw, and the man at the camera, who might need to know how to slide a foreground cel leftward faster than a central cel which slid faster than the background ("I've used as many as three layers for certain effects," says Jones) just to get, on a Warner budget, the kind of shifting-perspective look they were used to getting over at Disney with the megabuck Multiplane camera.[3] And that inventory omits, among other skills, the bizarre

3. True, at Warners they weren't getting differential focus, the plane of emphasis sharp, other planes fuzzed. Which also means they weren't getting an attention-distractor, which, alas, describes much of what Disney spent money on.

skills of Treg Brown, than whom no one was more resourceful at making the ear hear what the eye wasn't seeing. "When
the Coyote got his foot caught in the line attached to a harpoon and was dragged willy-nilly across the desert floor over
cacti, under boulders, bumping and slapping every obstacle
possible, never once did Treg supply a logical sound effect:
flying springs, breaking bottles, small explosives, human
ouch'es and oof's, popping balloons, railroad crossing bells,
and so on." That was *Zoom and Bored* (1957), where things
went too fast for an audience to ever quite realize it couldn't
possibly be hearing what it was seeing. Nor did Treg *need*
arrays of equipment; with merely a newspaper he could create the sound of "any kind of fire from bon- to forest to
rocket."[4] Imagine a recording session at Termite Terrace. No,
it's not a sane milieu we're hinting at.

Understandably, even principal characters, the only studio
properties to command an audience's awareness, developed
mild cases of multiple personality. Bugs Bunny evolved out
of a collective uncertainty, "moving from director to director,
picking up and dropping comic turns and comedic character-
istics of possible use to the mature character. But none of this
was deliberate. We not only didn't know that there was a
comic genius brewing in our group, we didn't even know we
were pregnant."[5] The famous name, even, was accidental. In
1938, when almost the only well-defined Termite Terrace
character was Porky Pig, a director who answered to Bugs
Hardaway, though his formal name was Ben, thought a rabbit might play nicely opposite Porky, and commissioned one
from the resident character designer. The designer, a Disney
alumnus named Charles Thorson, sent back a model sheet

4. *Chuck Amuck,* p. 191.
5. *Chuck Amuck,* p. 195.

headed "Bugs' bunny." ("Had it been for me," Jones remarks, "it would have been 'Chuck's bunny.' " Also the label would have been forgotten. Who it was had the genius to perceive the fitness of "Bugs" no one seems to remember.) Hardaway's film, *Porky's Hare Hunt,* featured a rounded nervous rabbit, crouched, always ready to leap for an exit; but "the Bugs that evolved," Chuck Jones remarks, "stood upright, a guy who's not going to go anyplace—sure of himself."[6] The Hardaway Bugs, though, did utter one enduring line: "Of course you realize this means war." As 1938 audiences would have known, it's a steal from Groucho Marx.

A Wild Hare (1940) was Tex Avery's consolidation. Not only have we for the first time Elmer Fudd's "Be vewy, vewy quiet, I'm hunting wabbits!" and Bugs's sharp "What's up, Doc?" we have also, as Friz Freleng remembers, something utterly new: "A rabbit so cocky that he wasn't afraid of a guy with a gun who was hunting him." All connection with timidity, with cuteness, is severed. And here's a moment to remark that Warner Bros. features, such as drew audiences to the theaters where Warner Bros. cartoons were shown, were (in Chuck Jones's words) "gentle pictures like *Little Caesar, I Was a Fugitive from a Chain Gang, Dr. Ehrlich's Magic Bullet.*" They starred the likes of Humphrey Bogart, James Cagney, George Raft. Their visual style featured murk and mist and fast cutting between short violent scenes. That was no milieu at all for a cute bunny, and by 1946 (in Freleng's *Racketeer Rabbit*) Bugs was reducing to panic co-stars the likes of Edward G. Robinson. ("Help! Police! Don't leave me with that crazy rabbit!")[7]

6. Joe Adamson, *Bugs Bunny: Fifty Years and Only One Grey Hare* (1990), p. 53.
7. Adamson, *Bugs Bunny,* p. 47.

Who's in Charge Here?

Anyhow, after *A Wild Hare* "all we had to do" (Jones recalls) "was to follow Tex's lead. The only problem was, none of us knew or could figure out what Tex had done right. Including Tex." Bugs might have settled into a personality derived from Harpo and Groucho—alternately the knowing innocent and the slinger of zingers—had Avery not left for MGM, leaving Freleng and Jones and McKimson and Clampett to reflect that the Bunny they had at Warners was "gradually becoming a more complex character" which it behooved them to shape. That's sensitive in divining that though Bugs had no visible or commercial existence save as they drew him and timed him, still it was important—hence meaningful—to think of a Bugs whose autonomy they were obliged to respect.[8] "Bugs went through a period of wild awkwardness before settling into the self-contained studied attitudes peculiar to him, so that his every movement is Bugs and Bugs only, just as his speech developed from a kind of vaudevillian patois loaded with 'deses' and 'doses' to a fully cadenced speech in which he studiously inserts an occasional 'ain't' in the same casual way as an Oxford graduate does."[9] In sum, "We discovered the enormous difference between being crazy—as in *A Wild Hare*—and playing at being crazy."

This goes deep; I'll permit myself two more paragraphs of quotation: "In short, all fat had to be removed from his dialogue, his figure, and his behavior. We were, in volleying Bugs back and forth from director to director, developing the heart and muscles of a mature and believable character.

---

8. Chuck Jones recalls a child correcting her father: "Mr. Jones doesn't draw Bugs Bunny. He draws *pictures of* Bugs Bunny."

9. *Chuck Amuck,* pp. 199–200. (A clarification: when Avery left Warners, McKimson was an animator there, not yet a director.)

"I think we all would have been embarrassed if one of us had tried to state what was happening in philosophical or logical terms. Logic and philosophy were certainly there, underlying the growth of our characters. But we were shy of pontification as well as of aesthetic theorizing or critique. Only in retrospect can we see that there was a deep and innocent knowledge forming within this heterogeneous and varied crew, and that knowledge produced the atmosphere for all the other characters who grew to maturity during those same years, between 1941 and 1950, and beyond. During those years we learned what was funny without analyzing *why* it was funny, and, even more important, what was *not* funny."

That last sentence is tricky. Does "learned" govern the two "what" clauses—we learned what was funny and what wasn't? Or does "what was *not* funny" go with *"why* it [what was funny] was funny," as one of a contrasting pair we learned not to analyze? That's worth spelling out just to indicate that we've somehow wandered into a semantic forest. How to talk about characters who never "really" existed, like Bugs or Achilles, characters moreover who cannot be assigned to a sole inventing intelligence such as Shakespeare's, is a question lit crit doesn't know how to confront. And what's to be done with the undeniable fact that Bugs—say —although the property of millions of viewers, was also the creation of (at a simplification) at least four directors, all of whom used somewhat different model sheets and had somewhat different conceptions of who Bugs would be if he were human (though stubbornly, he'd remain a penciled rabbit)?

Jones is explicit about the origin of his personal Bugs. "I could not animate a character I could laugh at but could not understand. A wild wild hare was not for me; what I needed was a character with the spicy, somewhat erudite introspection of a Professor Higgins, who, when nettled or threatened, would respond with the swagger of D'Artagnan as played by Errol Flynn, with the articulate quick-wittedness of Dorothy Parker—in other words, the Rabbit of My Dreams."

Such a Bugs—and note how *literary* are the analogies— "is far too strong a character to behave as an early Daffy Duck or a late Woody Woodpecker acts. It is no part of his character to go out and bedevil anyone for mischief's sake alone."

Hence: "*Golden Rule.* Bugs must always be provoked."[10]

Jones makes his case for rule-based comedy in the tenth, or Road Runner, chapter of *Chuck Amuck,* where he quotes Groucho Marx: "Comedy is not so much what you do, as what you don't do." Rules itemize the impermissibilities. On page 225 he lists "some of the rules" for the Coyote–Road Runner series (forty-two films at least: between four and five hours of screen time). They include: "No outside force can harm the Coyote—only his own ineptitude or the failure of the Acme products," and "No dialogue ever, except 'Beep-Beep!' " and "Whenever possible, make gravity the Coyote's greatest enemy." It's also specified that the Coyote could stop any time—*if* he were not a fanatic. To this, Santayana's definition of the Fanatic is appended: One who redoubles his effort, having forgotten his aim. For it's clear, Jones points out, that after the first couple of films the Coyote has utterly forgotten that his quest concerned something to eat. George Santayana was a genial philosopher who'd have been tickled to know that in *The Life of Reason* (1905–6) he'd inscribed a formula for an obsessed coyote.[11]

10. *Chuck Amuck,* p. 211.

11. The exact quotation: "Fanaticism consists in redoubling your efforts when you have forgotten your aim." As usual, Jones relies on memory to preserve the gist.

And why transfer that maxim to a *faux* animal kingdom?
Because (1) what can easily be done in live action, such as
human behavior, is specifically *not* the domain of animation;
(2) "It is easier to humanize animals than it is to humanize
humans," a dark saying philosophers would be rotating end-
lessly had they received it from a sixteenth-century Mon-
taigne instead of from a Spokane-born movie-maker whose
specialties have included mock-coyotes, mock-rabbits,
mock-ducks.[12] Maxim 1 is specifically where a Termite Ter-
racer peels away from Disney assumptions. As we've already
suggested, "the illusion of life" was a slogan that loaded the
huge Disney enterprise with dead ends: immense sums
squandered on making the "humans" in *Cinderella* (1950) and
Sleeping Beauty (1959) look as if live actors had been filmed, as
they likely should have been. If you're animating, then take
pencil in hand and *animate!* Don't restrict yourself to what a
clicky-click tripod-supported optical eavesdropper might
have picked up without even thinking (because it can't think)
about trying.

The Road Runner saga, all four-plus hours of it, relies on
just one theme, seemingly inexhaustible. That is Wile E.
Coyote's persistence in pursuit of what was once a potential
snack and has long since mutated into an ideal conquest. The
viewer of a new installment has seen all of it before and yet
seen none of it before. The setting is always an idealized
American southwest, paradise of bluffs and canyons and vast
spaces. Trucks or freight trains intrude sparingly, their
human denizens never visible. Also mail brings wares of the
Acme Company, which invariably malfunction. (But not
grossly; no, subtly. The defect that sends the Coyote yet one

12. For details see *Chuck Amuck*, pp. 227–9.

more time off the cliff is as minute as the programming error that can cost NASA yet another satellite.) And the fall off the cliff is so ritualized there is even a ritual explosion, a chemical madness of flame and orange clouds. That's especially evident in view of the normal Jones-Noble policy of reusing nothing.

So spare were the resources, so scant the need for normal chores such as designing new settings, that when *What's Opera, Doc?*, the most visually ambitious of all the studio's thousand-odd shorts, was estimated at seven weeks' drawing and shooting time instead of the normal five—104 separate "shots" as against the usual 60-odd—it was sandwiched be-

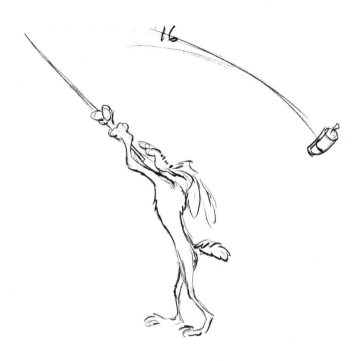

Who's in Charge Here?

tween a pair of Road Runners which could be brought off in four weeks apiece. On the time-sheets that went to Accounting, the total of fifteen weeks was allotted evenly.

Men continually learning to do what they were doing—that's not a bad way to describe an animation crew in those golden years. And a reflexive look at what they were learning to do—that helps account for *Duck Amuck (1953),* which is also indebted to *Sherlock Jr.* (1924): Buster Keaton playing a projectionist who wanders down the movie-house aisle and into the movie he's projecting. There he becomes "the immediate victim of whatever way the scenes happen to be cut. As he sets foot in the living room, the scene cuts and instantly he is outside at the entrance door. He knocks—cut—and then falls off the steps. The steps have disappeared. He is now in a garden."[13]

You get the idea. Daffy Duck, unlike Buster, got it too, and it roused him to mounting levels of indignation. As far as Keaton could tell, his problem was simply with The Way Things Were; hence his look of dreamy bemusement. Daffy's though, was with an enemy he could get mad at: an Animator, an omnipotence whose eraser destroyed each set for which Daffy was costumed, and whose paintbrush again and again brought into being, as easily as in the Book of Genesis, a world for which Daffy was totally unequipped.

To think of Keaton is to remember Chaplin, who was, as it seems easy to overlook, a wholly different kind of artist. Chaplin was a great *performer,* whose performance the camera observed, chin leaning on palm. Any glitch in the performance it simply recorded, occasionally, if rarely, to Chaplin's regret. In *The Great Dictator* Hitler, as impersonated by Chap-

13. Rudi Blesh, *Keaton* (1966), pp. 245–6.

ally a Disney strength. Mickey, Minnie, Donald, Pluto—
their identity is chiefly visual. Of the Seven Dwarfs, Doc and
Grumpy and Dopey may claim character; Happy, Sleepy,
Sneezy and Bashful exhibit mannerisms. But the rule-based
Termite Terrace identities, those were creations with something—yes, granted, just a little, but *something*—in common
with the likes of Hamlet. For (1) there were things they
would or wouldn't do, and (2) what they would do, when
they did it, they did with a style we take pleasure in identify-
ing, a style of moving and talking that's continuous with
their look. Reflect that though Donald Duck is white and
wears a sailor jacket, Daffy is black and naked and—what?
"Neurotic" is a forceless word to set against Daffy's id-like
reserves of energy. "Thurvival of the fittest! . . . and besides
. . . it's fun!"—that's his idiot screech once he thinks he's
arranged for Elmer Fudd to shoot Bugs Bunny (*Rabbit Fire*,
1951). What makes the next bit work is Bugs's contemplative
calm: "(*Bites . . . crunch, crunch, crunch*) (*Mouth full*) Say, Doc
(*chew, chew*) are you tryin' to get yourself in trouble with the
law? This ain't wabbit-huntin' season . . ." No, it's *duck*-hunt-
ing season, something Daffy is quick to call "an inmitigated
frabication." We can hear his nerve crumbling, though after a
frenzied set of exchanges he attempts to take charge, with
these fateful words: "*I* say it's *duck season* and I say *Fire!!*" In
the next frame his bill has somehow been (as the dialogue
sheet notes) "blown askew," a mild phrase for its new geom-
etry. It's like him, to get so caught up in the vehement
rhythm of *Duck season! Wabbit season!* that he gives the order
to *Fire!!* just one luckless step out of phase.[18] And it's like

18. *Chuck Amuck*, p. 131.

Elmer Fudd, to be so scrupulous about matching the victim to the season, once he's satisfied he understands what season it is.

We say "It's like him" about folk we're confident we understand, and the major Termite Terrace characters inspire that order of confidence. Why is that true of Warner Bros. and of no other cartoon studio? Surely it's traceable to the Warner policy of putting a single director in sole charge. That the three directors who might manage Daffy or Bugs in a given season had each of them a slightly different slant seems to have enriched, rather than muddled, the lifelikeness of the characters. And that one of those directors brought to bear on animation as detached, as conceptual a mind as did Charles M. Jones: that unlikely fact has much to do, surely, with the evident superiority, year after year, of the Warner shorts. To risk a stark generalization: after *Snow White* (1937) had pioneered the animated feature, the Disney shorts are seldom memorable; an exception such as *Toot, Whistle, Plunk and Boom* (1953) is apt to bear the hallmark of a virtuoso director (here, Ward Kimball). Elsewhere? For thirteen years MGM had the great Tex Avery; after 1940 they also had Hanna and Barbera putting Tom and Jerry through their formulaic wars. Those differ from the Coyote–Road Runner quest in that whereas Wile E. and his quarry exist in different psychic universes—the one obsessed, the other blithe—the Tom-and-Jerry formula calls simply for a cat who'd eat a mouse if only he could manage to catch it; but the mouse, being smaller, hence smarter, can always outmaneuver him. The Road Runner *never* outmaneuvers the Coyote. He's never even distressed by him. What outdoes the Coyote is the interactiveness of a single coherent universe, where fanaticism is guaranteed to defeat itself. True, that's not such a universe as defeated Hitler, but it sustains forty-two cohesive six-minute cartoons. And so on and so forth, and do not even mention Woody Woodpecker. No, as Disney short cartoons faded it was Termite Terrace or nothing.

Also, Termite Terrace could build on its own history. It's been noted that when a gunman threatened Jack Benny with "Your money or your life!" and Jack hesitated a countable number of seconds before muttering that he was trying to decide, his hesitation, and the resultant laughter, built on years of establishing a character, Jack the Tightwad. Likewise, by the time of *The Merry Wives of Windsor* Shakespeare's audiences knew what to expect of Jack Falstaff. Likewise too, by the time of *What's Opera, Doc?* (1957), a masterpiece as *The Merry Wives* is not, privileged audiences know that when the figure who casts huge shadows on orange cliffs turns out to be Elmer Fudd, they're simultaneously regarding a Fuddy emulation of the demon through whom *Fantasia* dramatized Mussorgsky's violent music, and watching one more Fuddian attempt at grandiosity (a *Heldentenor?* spare us), and coping with an inept impersonation of Siegfried, and engaged with yet another episode of "Kill the wabbit!" That's four layers at least; it resembles a piling-up of cels. Much, back in '57, could depend on your neighborhood. If you lived near a theater owned by Warner Bros. you'd likely seen enough Warner cartoons to enjoy the habitué's response; but if your cartoon fare had been chiefly Disney, or Tom and Jerry, then the *What's Opera, Doc?* you saw was something quite different, brilliant but arbitrary. And when Brünnhilde made an entrance, impersonated by gray-furred Bugs in a Marilyn Monroe pose, a-grin atop a bulky, self-conscious white horse with eye-makeup and a flowered garland, then—But wait! That horse!!

After more than a third of a century Jones is rightly proud of that horse. It's huge, like Wagnerian divas; also white, and rectangular, and smug. Detail by detail it's "beautiful," but the sum of exquisite parts is a cumbersome rectangle. That rectangularity cries out to be dwelt on. The Rectangle bobs to and fro; tiny Legs support and propel it. A smug expression indicates that all aspects of locomotion have been seen to (and Bugs looks confident that he'll not be tossed off). Bugs slides down the horse's back and neck, and, next thing we know, he and Elmer are engaged in a ballet. A ballet! Good grief, a horse that deposits you in a ballet! "Tatiana Riabouchinska and David Lichine were unwitting contributors to the authenticity of this bit of terpsichore," runs an enigmatic caption in *Chuck Amuck*.[19] It means, Footage of a

19. *Chuck Amuck*, p. 207. And the five color illustrations in this spread merit loving study.

performance of theirs was studied by the animating team. The music heard by viewers of the animation was performed by the Burbank Symphony, which was under instructions to eschew any clowning. The film has 104 "cuts"—i.e., wholly new setups—in just over six minutes. That's about twice the usual count, which helps explain something we've already noticed, billable time filched from adjacent Road Runners.

Whether Wagner's fame can hope for shelter is another question. In 1989, at Northwestern University, a professor of music history informed a survey class of music seniors that this week's subject would be the *Ring* cycle. All forty students promptly burst into a massive Valkyrie-esque rendition of "Kill the wabbit!"

The end came, though Chuck Jones still thinks it needn't have. In 1962 the Brothers Warner closed down the cartoon operation.[1] They'd done that previously in 1953,[2] when Jack W. mistook a fad for a trend and decided that all films would thenceforth be 3-D. He saw that as ominous because 3-D, requiring separate frames for the left and right eye, would run the cost of animation up unthinkably. But the alarm was false (anyone here *remember* 3-D?), and after four months, which Chuck Jones spent over at Disney doing next to nothing, a nine-year respite ensued at Warners. In those last golden years Jones would create such masterpieces as *What's Opera, Doc?* and *One Froggy Evening,*

1. But not before making one 3-D cartoon, *Lumberjack Rabbit,* directed by Jones.
2. Misdated in *Chuck Amuck* (p. 277) as 1955.

also wonders like *Broom-Stick Bunny* and some of the finest Road Runners, notably *Gee Whiz-z-z-z* and *Zoom and Bored,* the one with the huge errant harpoon.

At the end, '62, what had happened wasn't 3-D but, Chuck Jones thinks, quite simply, TV. This time doom really was written on the wall. Annual American expenditure on movie tickets had, very suddenly, halved. Folks were sitting at home, mutating into couch potatoes. Hence the end of the historic two-hour package—Newsreel, Cartoon, Short, ninety-minute feature—the whole "block-booked" into a theater that just ordered the feature. So features got longer (most features now contain thirty minutes of padding.) And newsreel and cartoon and short all disappeared.

Jones talks as if the studios simply gave up too easily. For mightn't people have chosen the movie they'd see tonight with an eye for such garnishings as the cartoon? But viewers weren't offered such a choice, mainly because in 1948 Paramount lost a Supreme Court antitrust case. That put an end to the studio-owned theater chains, the chains that had kept block-booking active—as it were, all in the family—after independent theater owners had pretty well gotten themselves exempted from it. So when TV became a sudden threat the studio chains weren't there any more to support a counteroffensive, and block-booking, which had survived as a convenient habit, was suddenly passé.[3]

And that seemed to be an end for Winsor McCay's 1914 creation, because if there was no demand for animation why trouble to do it?

3. For a too-brief account see Gerald Mast, *A Short History of the Movies* (5th ed., 1992). There should be a fuller exposition but I've not run across one.

Well, every craft designates some earlier craft as an "Art," which it proceeds to package so as to enhance its own plausibility. ("I may be cardboard, but I bring you jewels.") In the '30s movies packaged books. Filming *Tom Sawyer* and *David Copperfield* had the purpose of legitimizing movies, which until they offered *books* (understood to be good for you) were simply occasions for kids to waste time. In the process, marginal things like *Anne of Green Gables* got legitimized as "literature" by becoming movies.

Then, starting in the '50s, video (what you saw on the home screen) was packaging movies (what you'd formerly seen on the large one). That was meant to help you take TV seriously, but an odd side-effect was to turn "movie" into "cinema": Thus *every filmed thing* now merited scrutiny! Another result was to rescue marginal ciné phenomena, such as animation, for intent attention. That could take a while; as we've noted, *Time's* Jay Cocks discovered Chuck Jones as late as 1973, and the trailblazing animation issue of *Film Comment* ("Published by the Film Society of Lincoln Center") didn't appear till early 1975. The mills of the academic gods do, sure enough, grind, but oh, how they can grind slowly!

By 1975 Chuck Jones was 63 and well on the way to defining a second career. He'd moved to MGM, done some thirty-five Tom-and-Jerrys[4] with which he still doesn't feel comfortable, and in 1965 had somehow managed *The Dot and the Line,* a tour-de-force which won an Oscar.[5] It's worth a digression.

4. That's counting some he produced but didn't direct.
5. Previously, several nominations had won him just two, both in 1950. One was for a Pepé Le Pew, the other for a Public Health Service documentary, *So Much for So Little.*

Character Animation, by the Jones definition, expresses—delimits—Character by Way-of-Moving, not by mere Appearance. Back in '33, you'll remember, Disney's pigs looked alike but were different "people" because they moved differently. Wile E. Coyote, whose career began in 1949, is who he is thanks to all manner of angular compressions. Even in his way of crashing down from a cliff he's no Elmer, no Daffy, no Bugs. And what might be done with even less than a coyote? In 1960 Jones and Maltese and Ken Harris and the Usual Termite Terrace Suspects had come up with *High Note,* about a note who seems—like all the other characters—indistinguishable from any other note on a sheet of music, but who's "high" because he hangs out where they're playing "Little Brown Jug," and hence keeps missing his *Blue Danube* cue. A

After Warners

drunk and rebellious delinquent, an imperious conductor, a suite of melodious *Blue Danube* notes who'd not dream of doing anything out of tune or sequence—such are the personnel of a cartoon with no dull moments, situated in a space wholly defined by staves and clefs. (Jones had meant it to be monochrome, but Eddie Selzer insisted on the color he paid for.)

Well, that was still at Warner Bros., and a splendid instance of what the Warner system could permit if not encourage. (*High Note* even got nominated for an Oscar, but failed to gratify Eddie Selzer by winning one.) *The Dot and the Line,* which did win one for MGM, is still more abstract. Its "characters" are, yes, one Dot and one Line, also one Squiggle. ("I associated completely with the line!" Jones would claim in 1980.)[6] Its source is a book by Norton Juster, about a Dot and a Line, subtitled "A Romance in Lower Mathematics." In Charles Solomon's summary, "The disciplined, purposeful straight line defeats a boorish, ragged squiggle to win the heart of the flighty magenta dot."[7] Juster seems to have attracted Chuck Jones by the sheer abstractness of his conceptions. (For run it by again: A *book* about a Dot and a Line!)

Another Juster book, *The Phantom Tollbooth,* underlay Jones's one venture (1971) into feature-length animation. "A critical success," he remarks, "a box-office question mark." He adds that it tends to resurface at film festivals.[8]

Fortunately available on videotape, it offers some utterly amazing animation. Try the "Doldrums" sequence early on:

6. Interview with Joe Adamson, in *The American Animated Cartoon* (1980), ed. Danny Peary and Gerald Peary.

7. Charles Solomon, *The History of Animation* (1989), p. 264.

8. *Chuck Amuck,* p. 278.

green apathetic froggish beings oozing down every available surface—notably the windshield of Milo's car—lured by the simple delights of indolence in the Primal Ooze. Milo is a boy say ten years old, and as to what he's doing with a car—well, the Juster book does explain it, and so does the film; but what's Chuck Jones doing with that book?

Chuck Jones is doing what he does so often, revisiting his own boyhood. *Chuck Amuck* begins with an enchanting chapter about the lessons imparted, oh, back when C. J. was seven, by a cat named Johnson. That's the chapter that cites Joyce's transcription of cat-speech, and also cites Mark Twain's statement that if you carried a cat home by the tail you would get information that would be valuable to you all your life.[9] Put that chapter alongside the simple fact that the Jones who'd read so many books, and would enroll in the Chouinard Art Institute, never did finish high school, and we have a type rare these days: a demonstrably brilliant kid driven out of his mind not by peer pressure but by sheer classroom boredom. Jones based at least a couple of Warner films on such a kid, for instance, *From A to Z-Z-Z-Z* (1954), in which a boy named Ralph fantasizes more interesting things than the teacher seems to be saying. "Forced to answer a math problem, he believes the numbers are laughing at him so he becomes a white-on-black chalkboard figure and fights with the doodle-figures, improvising letters as weapons."[10]

Letters as weapons against Numbers—that is a fallacy the numerate encounter time and again ("I can't balance a check-

9. It's worth preserving the detail that whenever Chuck, as often, said something oracular his Warner colleagues chose to assume he was quoting Mark Twain.

10. Jerry Beck and Will Friedwald, *Looney Tunes and Merrie Melodies* (1989), p. 266.

book," some *Hamlet* expert will boast), as also do the literate ("Too fuzzy to consider," brags the Euclid guru on being confronted with Shakespeare). Such is a central theme of *The Phantom Tollbooth,* in which two beautiful princesses, Sweet Rhyme (words) and Pure Reason (math), need rescuing from a Castle in the Air. Their rescuer will be Milo; and he, like (presumably) Chuck Jones at a similar age, was finding classroom procedures boring. In the early minutes of the film a live-action Milo can barely be bothered to drag himself home from school; we may note a family resemblance to the Ralph of *From A to Z-Z-Z-Z.* Then (ZAP!!!) a mysterious package arrives: a Tollbooth, and a neat red car for driving through Tollbooths. Hence Milo's heroic journey. For most of it he's abetted by a dog who's named Tock because he's a (Tick Tock, get it?) "watch" dog. That's an order of whimsy the script inherits from Juster's book, on the pages of which such word-play works better than it does on-screen. What holds the strange film together—and it *does* hold together—is Maurice Noble's visual design and the Chuck Jones direction. (The Abe Levitow who's credited as co-director was a major animator on Chuck Jones's team in the Warner days.) The transition between Live Action and Animation is especially fine. Again and again Milo, trying things out, runs the red car leftward (into the animated world), then back rightward (into the photographed one), and on the left of the Tollbooth his animated leg will wave, but simultaneously on its right his realistic arm. That situates Milo in both worlds at once. By the time the film has committed itself to Animation, there's no doubt that the two worlds are equally substantial, what's effected *here,* amid things hand-drawn, entraining consequences back *there,* where a camera merely picks up happenings.

After Warners

In an earlier chapter we saw Jones in his Warner days endorsing the principle that if you want live action you should go film it, not torment animators into confecting some Illusion of Life. *The Phantom Tollbooth* is a perfect illustration. Bored schoolboy Milo needn't be hand-drawn, and isn't; he's played by a kid named Butch Patrick, in a live-action world with its own live-action director (David Monahan). But adventurer Milo is the work of animators, like the world he adventures in, a world designed by Maurice Noble and drawn, under Jones and Levitow, by a very talented crew. It's in passing through the Phantom Gate, say A.D. 1960, that the bored Milo becomes the adventurer, as it was in sea-passage through the bounds of deepest water, say 1000 B.C., that Odysseus the beset mariner became the Odysseus who had intercourse with shades. Odysseus paid his toll, a black bellsheep, as Milo pays his, an American coin.

And if Odysseus and Milo are some three millennia apart, it's invigorating to reflect how persistent are a few basic themes. The theme here is a journey into a world with different parameters, but a world from which you may expect to return. Odysseus went to the underworld because Circe warned him that if he didn't he'd never achieve what he yearned for, the sight of home. Next—eight or nine centuries later—Vergil sent his Aeneas into a different underworld because until he went there he'd not achieve his destiny, which was to found Rome. Next, Dante (A.D. 1300, an ideal date) sent his own alter ego, with Vergil for guide, on a long journey, the reward of which would be, oh, the salvation of one Italian soul, but mainly the edification and delight of readers whose numbers there's no estimating, and of whom many cannot even read his Italian.

For all arts above a certain level of seriousness—here Character Animation can sometimes qualify—draw on a common stock of images and situations. So do not be surprised to meet Homer's people in a Jones's or a Juster's domain. Norton Juster (b. 1929) "studied architecture at the University of Pennsylvania, city planning at the University of Liverpool on a Fulbright scholarship, and spent three years as a legal officer, personnel officer, and education officer in the U.S. Navy, stationed in Morocco and Newfoundland."[11] That's, yes, the sort of life-story that might tumble someone's mind into a space athwart Homer. *The Dot and the Line* was published by Random House in 1961, with some one hundred illustrations by Jules Feiffer, whose not-inexpensive presence meant that the publishers were, rightly, serious. "One of the most popular children's books of the '60s," says a blurb on the videotape.

Still, it's not your standard Saturday-matinee kid-fare, and despite well-intentioned burbles from the *New York Times* ("Perfectly dandy and altogether engaging") the great public seems no more to have been engaged than it has been, more recently, by rumors that its members' bodies are all assembled from quarks. (Let's face it, moreover: would *you* pay to see a film because a newspaper had come up with the wimp phrase "Perfectly dandy"?)

It's clear that by 1971 no one had any idea what an eighty-nine-minute stretch of animation might be good for. That doesn't bear on what you or I may see in it today on videotape. It bears on whatever it was that might have brought crowds (as in *Snow White* days) into neighborhood cinemas. That seems not to have been workable in 1971, but it's become possible again in the 1990s, in part, as we've already noted, because feature-scale animation is actually cheaper

11. Jacket blurb to *The Phantom Tollbooth* (Random House, 1961).

now than live action. Get a surefire story like the Disney *Beauty and the Beast* or *Aladdin,* decorate the likes of the latter with a star like Robin Williams, and you've still lots of cash left over for promotion. But in 1971 the costs, in relation to live action, were high. Also, *The Phantom Tollbooth* was not a well-known story, let alone a story easy to promote. What did work in '71, and had worked as early as 1967, was the TV special. Chuck Jones's first venture into that medium was the '67 *How the Grinch Stole Christmas,* a wonderful half-hour film that still gets annual showings.

But a problem with the TV special (twenty-six minutes, allowing for commercial time) is that by classic Warner Bros. standards (six minutes, ZAP) we've a *lot* of screen time to fill up: between four and five times the length of a Looney Tune. But a story that many times more intricate than the story of *One Froggy Evening* is not conceivable. So we can't solve our problem with a trickier story. We'll have to alter Pace and Timing.

Which is what we do; and—especially with the altering of pace—we find we're defining a whole different quality of attention. Remember, at Warner Bros. we didn't have to establish a character like Bugs Bunny in just one film, the way we now have to establish the Grinch. Having to do that does make a difference—and consumes time. The Jones Grinch is peculiar to just this picture, whereas a Bugs, or a Daffy, transcends any special application. We'll be devoting a lot of work to the Grinch, and part of the viewers' pleasure will be getting to know him.

Also, the Dr. Seuss book about the grumpy Grinch can entertain much younger children than would be able to follow *Rabbit Seasoning.* Story and characters being simple alike, pleasure, for older viewers as for the youngest, is going to

flow from the easy-to-share complications of doing simple
things. It's altogether appropriate that during one screening
of a key scene, when the dynamics of a sled poised to head
down the wrong side of a mountain are engaging our neuro-
muscular anxieties because the on-screen characters aren't
quite tall enough to reposition it easily, one Jones connois-
seur[12] should have remarked, "If he couldn't draw, he would
have been a physicist."

That's as accurate an assessment of Chuck Jones as has
ever been made. The sled, grotesquely overloaded, is precari-
ously balanced on that peak, and where it's headed—down
to Grinchy Oblivion? or back to where its stolen contents
can be put where they belong?—has become the whole
point of the film. "Point": Euclid called that "a position without magnitude," not denying that it can contain all possible
directions ("vectors").[13] And at this high moment the frantic
moral struggle becomes, for us in the audience, neuromuscu-
lar, because we're twitching our shoulders leftward, wanting
the sled to head *that*-away, back down toward the Children
of Whoville. Yes, physics is one occupation Chuck Jones
might have followed. Vectors, and our ability to internalize
vectors, were (minus such names) built into his nervous system. Any competent animator can lean an instability rightward. Not many can do that while also making a whole audience join in trying to lurch it leftward. (True, the fact that the
narrative voice was Boris Karloff's didn't hurt a bit.)

Then (1975) there was *Rikki-Tikki-Tavi,* with its art of the
post-retinal image. Rikki's way of getting on-screen and off-

12. Robert Kenner, magazine editor, in December 1991.
13. Vector: an action pointed for a measured trip toward a specified somewhere. (Tip the sled, and tip it *that* way, for a descent *that* far.)

screen: would you believe that would be a prime way to characterize him, also a prime memory for viewers? It's a great achievement, analogous to enchanting a reader of prose by your use of the definite article. Yes, what we're seeing in the TV years is Jones occupied with the bare bones of his craft: the unbalanced sled of *The Grinch,* the enter/exit of Rikki, or the movement repertoire of the cat named Harry in *A Very Merry Cricket* (1973), who is far superior to his predecessor, the sleek cat in *The Cricket in Times Square.*

But the half-hour TV specials fade away too. Let's face it, the Jones way of doing them—"full" vs. "limited" animation—is expensive. And, stories being in limited supply, it always seems smarter to rerun, any Christmas, the classic *Grinch.* No, it's clear that the real Jones medium was the full-animation six-minute cartoon, just as Joseph Conrad's medium wasn't the novel but something of say ninety pages, the length of *Heart of Darkness.* The disappearance of the kind of magazine that used things of that length left Conrad stranded, needing to pad things out. (The "short story" likewise hasn't survived the demise of the likes of the *Saturday Evening Post,* so from a commercial hit it's turned into an art form.)

Yes, media matter. What called the commercial novel into existence was a market for book-length fictions that (unlike *Paradise Lost*) wouldn't be reread. They'd be skimmed and discarded, or handed to poor relations. And after people who worked in London began living elsewhere and commuting by train for perhaps two hours each way, a British firm named W. H. Smith made a fortune by divining that the place to sell books was the railway station.

Like the 60,000-word novel, the 6-minute cartoon derives its tautness from an economy imposed by commerce,

not art. Art can work within that economy. Chuck Jones—
let's face it—isn't at all at ease with half an hour at his disposal. In July 1993 he was talking with relief of an upcoming
Warner animation project in which he'd be main panjan-
drum, and—get this!—he'd negotiated a length limit, *six
minutes*.

Six minutes. Just what had been arrived at, all those aeons
ago, by tight-fisted Warner types head to head with tight-
fisted exhibitor types, hammering out what would be the defining criterion of a new kind of art.

After Warners

Index

Designer:	Steve Renick
Compositor:	ComCom
Text:	Monotype Columbus & Monotype Perpetua
Display:	Monotype Perpetua
Printer:	Haddon Craftsmen, Inc.
Binder:	Haddon Craftsmen, Inc.